Ethics

An Introduction to Moral Theory

Michael S. Russo

SophiaOmni

Third Edition

ISBN: 978-1493694495

SophiaOmni

Visit our website at:
www.sophiaomni.org

This book is dedicated to my students—past, present, and future—and to those amazing men and women I have been fortunate to know who have provided me with living illustrations of the moral life in action.

CONTENTS

preface

I know exactly what you're thinking: does the world really need yet another college textbook on ethics? I mean, after all, if you do a book search on Amazon.com and put in the word "ethics" you are likely to find more books on the subject than you can read in a lifetime. And the list of these books would include works like Aristotle's *Nicomachean Ethics* that were written centuries ago (and which are still relevant today) as well as more than a few works by some fairly impressive moral theorists that were published only within the past few years.

So why, then, is this short study of ethical theory necessary at the present time?

I'll pass over the fact that, given the persistent moral ambiguity that seems to reign supreme today, we probably can never have too many books published that help individuals clarify their own moral thinking. If anything, there is probably too little ethics being read and discussed in our own society rather than too much.

The real reason why I wrote this book is much more practical than that. You see, I've been teaching ethics for over twenty-five years now, and I've done so in a variety of settings. I've taught ethics in one form or another to junior high school students in the South Bronx, to prep school students at a prestigious Academy, and at several colleges and universities in both graduate and undergraduate programs. What I discovered over these twenty-five years is that most texts in ethics are written in a way that often fails to serve the most basic needs of the average eighteen-year-old, who may be sincerely looking for some degree of moral clarity in his or her own life.

These students come into ethics classes, often during their freshman or sophomore years of college, and encounter books which are chock full of complex theories, obscure language, obtuse case studies, and issues which often seem somewhat esoteric, to say the least.

Nor do many of these texts provide simple, straightforward guidance that can help typical college students with the complex issues that they have to face every day of their lives. The first years of college can often seem like a moral mine field in which young men and women are free for the first time to make decisions on their own, and have to live with the consequences of these decisions. I believe a text in ethics should serve as a resource tool that actually aids in the moral decision-making process.

That's the reason why I developed *Ethics: Living Sanely in an Insane World*. Among the features that I believe make this text different from others currently used in college ethics classes are the following:

It is short and easy to read. Most texts in ethics tend to be a bit long-winded because the authors of these texts and their publishers need to justify the high costs they charge to readers by adding more words. These texts also tend to be filled with complex jargon that can throw off the average reader. In an attempt to make the study of ethics as accessible as possible to the widest audience possible, I have intentionally made each chapter of this text as brief as possible while still allowing for a comprehensive discussion of the theories presented. I have also attempted to keep the technical philosophical verbiage that one often finds in typical ethics texts to a minimum. Where it has been necessary to use discipline-specific terms, I have attempted to explain these terms as clearly as possible so that they don't become stumbling blocks as you work your way through the text.

It focuses on down-to-earth issues. While many courses on ethics focus on the most dramatic and controversial issues—abortion, infanticide, war, etc.—I believe that the vast majority of moral dilemmas that individuals face occur in our ordinary everyday dealings with other human beings. It is for this reason that many of the examples and case studies in this text focus on everyday moral issues, particularly those likely to affect the average college student such as yourself.

It has a very specific goal in mind. The aim of this text, as I have already pointed out, is to assist you in developing your own framework for moral decision-making. I have focused most of this text on explaining five of the most influential moral theories in the history of Ethics—ethical egoism, utilitarianism, deontology, rights theory, and virtue ethics. By the end of the text you should be in a position to determine which of these theories—if any—makes the most sense to you and why. After that, it will be up to you to attempt to apply this theory as consistently as possible to your everyday moral decision-making.

This text would not have been possible without the contributions of several wonderful individuals who took time to proofread the completed work and offer many helpful suggestions. Allow me, therefore, to express my sincerest thanks to Marie Dollard, Laura Hefele, Una Milella, Elisa Rapaport, and Ashley Lantz for their assistance in producing this text.

WHY WE NEED ETHICS

Case Study: A Day in the Life

It is Tuesday morning around 7am. You got to bed late last night after an evening of partying with friends, and now you are having trouble getting up for your morning classes. Your alarm keeps blaring its warning to you that you are running late, but you keep hitting the snooze button for just a few more minutes of sleep.

You hear some pounding on the door and your mother's grating voice telling you that if you don't get up right now you will be late for your 8:15 accounting class. You manage to pull yourself up from bed, covering your ears to block out your mother's voice and in frustration scream out to her, "Shut the hell up and leave me alone for two minutes, will you!" She leaves in a huff, offended as usual by your abrupt morning behavior.

It is now 7:40 and you know you will have to rush if you are to make it to class on time. You quickly brush your teeth, shower, and get dressed. Before you leave the house, you stop into your older sister's bedroom on an important errand. Seeing that she has left already, you "borrow" $25 from the funds that she keeps in her dresser drawer, promising yourself that you will return this money after you get paid from work this evening.

Since you don't have time for a real breakfast, you stop off at 7-11 on the way to school and get some cigarettes and a large coffee, which lately has become your typical morning fare. Determined to get to class on time, you gulp your coffee, knock off a couple of cigarettes, search for the books you will need for class in the wasteland that is your car, all the while driving well above the speed-limit on the local expressway. No harm done though: there were no cops around today, so you made it through without getting a ticket, arriving on campus at exactly 8:15am.

Unfortunately, you didn't account for how long it would take you to find a parking space on campus and you arrive to class ten minutes late. As you enter the classroom, you can tell that the professor is annoyed that you are once again late for his class, but you pretend not to notice and slump into an available seat. You know that you should be paying attention to what he is saying—especially since the midterm is coming up soon—but you are so tired that your mind wanders aimlessly.

During a break in the class, you go into an empty stairwell with a classmate to smoke a cigarette. You bump into a friend named Karen, who is in your Philosophy of Existence class and ask her how she is doing on the paper for that class which is due on Thursday. Karen confesses that she simply bought a paper from an on-line academic paper site and that she is very happy with the results. Since you know that you will not have time to write a decent paper by Thursday, you get the web address of the site from Karen, determined to follow her example.

After class you bump into some of your friends hanging out in the cafeteria. They are talking about a mutual friend, who, it turns out, is pregnant and is considering having an abortion so she won't have to drop out of school. Although some of the people in the group clearly are concerned about their friend's welfare, most simply enjoy gossiping about her situation, speculating about the specific circumstances of her pregnancy. Delighting in the misfortunes of other people—they make your own life seem a little brighter in comparison—you offer up some particularly graphic information about this girl's sexual history that you heard about from one of her former boyfriends. Although this has nothing to do with her current predicament, your friends enjoy hearing all the sordid details you have to offer.

At 4:20pm you finish your classes for the day and head off for your job in the children's department of Macy's. Because you spent so much time gossiping, you are late once again, and, since the store manager already dislikes you intensely, you fear that you could very well lose your job. Fortunately, the assistant manager of the children's department is "really into you." Flirting outrageously with this lonely and pathetic individual, you con the assistant manager into covering for you with the hint of going out together at some point in the future. Of course you have no intention ever to do so. You spend the rest of the night trying to do as little work as possible, goofing off with your co-workers, and avoiding the store manager at all costs.

You end your day as you always do. Hanging out with your friends at one of their homes, drinking assorted alcoholic beverages, smoking some pot when it is available, and occasionally "hooking up" if the right person happens to come along.

For Discussion

Read through the above "typical day" in the life of a college student like yourself. Do any of the events or reactions described in this case study seem implausible to you (i.e., unlikely to happen to any real college student)? Which of the actions of the typical college student described would you characterize as morally problematic or wrong? What do you think it is that makes these acts wrong?

In the first case study in this text, you were offered a "typical day" of a fictitious college student. Of course the events described are compressed into a day to make the scenario a bit more interesting for you. I personally think that it would be rather unlikely that the average college student—even one as ethically challenged as the one portrayed in the case study—would make quite so many bad choices in such a short amount of time.

And yet, I also have no doubts that the kind of moral situations that our imaginary student faces are not at all unlike those which confront most college students at one point or another during the course of their everyday lives. I would go even further than this arguing that the moral choices that this student makes in the case study would probably be not unlike those that many college students would make in similar circumstances.

Our Moral Crisis

Perhaps you think that I am exaggerating the extent of moral confusion rampant in our colleges. In fact, college students are probably no more confused about the right way to live their lives than Americans in general. In study after study of ethical attitudes and beliefs, however, social scientists have detected an alarming decline of moral standards among average Americans. In one such study, James Patterson and Peter Kim surveyed 2000 people chosen at random about their moral attitudes. In their work, *The Day America Told The Truth* the authors shared the following statistics:

- Only 13% of Americans believe in all the Ten Commandments.

- 91 % of Americans lie regularly, at work and at home.
- 20% of women say they were raped by their dates.
- 33% of AIDS carriers have not told their spouses or lovers.
- 31 % of married people are having or have had an affair.
- 7% of participants say that for $2 million they would commit murder (Liszka 2).

One could argue that statistics like these are symptomatic of a deep moral crisis affecting Americans. Indeed, for many of us living at the beginning of the 21st century, it often appears as though the state of the world that we inhabit is about as morally bankrupt as it has ever been. Every time we open the newspaper or turn on the news, we are confronted with reports of corporate malfeasance, government corruption, sexual scandals, and assorted acts of cruelty and violence that boggle the mind.

Objectively, we have more than enough moral guidance in our daily lives to help us make the right moral choices. There are countless individuals around us—family, friends, co-workers—who are more than willing to tell us exactly how to live our lives, often bombarding us with their unique ideas about right and wrong, good and evil. If you go to any decent library or bookstore, you will find scores of books that have been written over the centuries by some pretty smart people in the field of ethics, trying to help us clarify our moral thinking. We are also constantly reminded of how we should behave by pulpit preachers, radio talk show hosts, and an eclectic collection of gurus and sages.

With all this help one would think that it would be relatively easy to figure out the right way to live our lives. And yet the sad fact is that more individuals than ever in our society are completely befuddled when it comes to making moral choices. The problem is not that we are making the wrong moral choices; the problem actually is that we don't have a framework in place for understanding what makes an act right or wrong in the first place. The average college student today probably believes that there is no objective basis for moral decisions and that the best one can do when confronted with a moral dilemma is to muddle one's way through it as best one can.

I do not wish to suggest that people weren't confused about moral matters in the past—of course they were—or that previous generations were more scrupulous in their moral practices than we are—of course they weren't. The difference is that although our grandparents might have had some questions about the right way to live their lives, they probably didn't doubt that there was a right way to live. And while they probably engaged in the same kinds of bad moral behavior that we do, at least they knew that they were behaving badly.

It appears that the unshakable certainties of previous generations have instead given way to disconcerting feelings of ambiguity. We no longer know what the right answers are to our moral dilemmas. We may even have a sense that we are living in a world where there are no longer any clear norms for moral behavior, a world in which each individual must look to him or herself to find the answers.

The Purpose of Ethics

Every day of our lives we are confronted with moral questions that demand answers. Some of these questions are fairly innocuous (whether, for example, to tell the truth or not to the telemarketer who calls during dinner and asks if you are home); other are significantly more complex (for instance, whether to cheat on your income taxes, have an abortion, or support government policies that may be unjust). The point here is that you just can't bury your head in the sand and pretend that these dilemmas don't exist or that they can just be imagined away.

It is precisely because each of us is confronted with so many difficult moral choices in our every day lives that the field of ethics becomes so very important. Ethics differs from most other fields of human inquiry in that the goal of studying about ethics is not simply to attain some sort of theoretical knowledge, but to acquire the kind of practical wisdom necessary to live a better life. Ethics may begin with theories, but always ends with how these theories can help clarify your moral decision-making process and ultimately help make you a more moral human being. As the philosopher Aristotle put it several centuries ago, "The purpose of [studying ethics] is not, as it is in other inquiries, the attainment of theoretical knowledge: we are not conducting this inquiry in order to know what virtue is, but in order to become good, else there would be no advantage in studying it." (*Nicomachean Ethics* II.2).

Fortunately, we don't have to solve all of our moral dilemmas completely on our own. Like any other complex field of human endeavor, ethics has its own set of "experts" who have struggled to find clear, consistent, and rational principles to guide human activity. When confronted with our own moral dilemmas, it is not always necessary to refer to what the great ethicist of the past and present have to say on these matters, but it may be comforting for you to know that there are thoughtful men and women who have reflected upon the same sorts of issues that you are facing, and may have some meaningful guidance to offer you as you attempt to sort through the moral issues that will undoubtedly arise throughout your life.

Finally, some individuals mistakenly presume that the purpose of ethics is to brainwash people into believing certain ideas about right and wrong. Nothing could be further from the truth. The purpose of ethics is to provide the broad theoretical framework to help you make intelligent moral decisions that fully reflect your own unique values and ideals. In the end what you choose to think or how you choose to act is entirely your own business.

Arguing Ethics...Civilly

There's one final thing you have to be prepared for now that you have chosen to undertake the study of ethics. Some students who enter ethics classes are put off by the argumentative nature of these classes. They might be coming from subjects like chemistry, math, or accounting, where there is very little debate at all over the topics being discussed. Then, when they enter their ethics classes, the kind of conversations that typically go on can often seem like a free-for-all.

Believe it or not, the fact that discussion, debate, and even vehement arguments are occurring in your ethics class is a good sign. It means that there is an honest, open exchange of ideas and that students feel comfortable enough to express their views candidly. Although this sort of dynamic exchange doesn't occur in every ethics class, it usually does in the best sorts of ethics classes—those in which faculty members are open to hearing students' ideas and the students themselves are intellectually invested in the subject matter.

Although debate is a natural feature of ethics classes, this debate should always be civil. As you read this text and discuss the topics found within it, there will undoubtedly be ideas presented by your classmates that you find silly, stupid, or even morally repugnant. Although it's perfectly fine to disagree with the moral positions of others, you should strive to do so in a way that is never demeaning or degrading.

Too often in our society the discussion of important ideas devolves into personal attacks that end in acrimony and discord. All this does is entrench individuals in their own partisan and dogmatic views, and nobody is enlightened as a result. While you can and should disagree with positions you find false—and disagree forcefully at that—ethics is also about being open to the possibility that you can learn something from those with whom you disagree. This doesn't mean that by giving the positions of opponents an honest hearing your own positions will change dramatically, or even at all. But your own moral perspective might very well be enhanced by exposure to ideas that you may not have considered before.

How to Use This Book

As I have previously mentioned, the aim of this work is not to turn you into some kind of preeminent scholar in the field of ethics (although that wouldn't be so bad); nor is it to provide you with esoteric ideas that you can use to dazzle your friends at the next party you attend (although that might actually make the party much more interesting). The aim of this work, quite simply and pragmatically, is to provide you with the tools you need to begin to live an ethical life.

You're probably thinking right now: "But I already am living a per-fectly moral life. So what on earth do I need to read a book like this for, anyway." In fact, you may be a terrific, kind-hearted, generous, and responsible person...But this doesn't necessarily mean that you are an ethical person. As you'll see throughout this book, living an ethical life presupposes that you understand the reasons why you behave the way you do, and, even more importantly, that you have certain clear, consis-tent, and rational principles that you follow when deciding how you are going to act in a particular situation. These are precisely the tools with which you will be provided as you work your way through the ideas be-ing presented.

To get the most out of this work, I would ask you to observe a few simple recommendations:

1. Each chapter of this text begins with a case study that typically involves an ordinary person just like yourself confronted with a moral situation that demands resolution. These case studies are intended to introduce the main ideas in each chapter and to illuminate your own attitudes and beliefs about these issues be-ing discussed. Make sure to read through these case studies and carefully reflect on the questions being posed by them *before*

reading the rest of the chapter.

2. As you read through the ideas and theories presented in each chapter, do so with a critical mind. No particular theory in the field of ethics is sacrosanct, and there is no theory without its own limitations. It is your job as a reader to assess the merits of each theory and then to consider how useful each of these theories may be if applied to your own life situation. It's my hope that, by the end of this text, you'll find at least one theory that resonates with you, and that you can begin to use to guide you when confronted with your own personal moral dilemmas.

3. Each chapter ends with exercises that help reinforce the theories that you have just read. Take the time to do these exercises and make sure you understand how each theory can be applied before moving on to the next theory. Remember, if you can't apply moral theories to concrete situations, these theories won't serve you very well in life.

4. For those who wish to delve more deeply into the ethical theories presented in this work, I've included a selection of primary sources at the end of the text that presents the ideas of some of the greatest thinkers in the field of ethics. You might find some of these selections a bit challenging, so you are advised to read them only after going through my basic overview of each moral theory in Part 2 of this text.

And above all else, try to have a good time!

For Further Discussion

1. Rank the following moral issues in terms of how important they are to you and using the following scale...

    VI = very important
    SI = somewhat important
    SU = somewhat unimportant
    VU = very unimportant

    _____ global poverty/hunger
    _____ overpopulation
    _____ war
    _____ global warming
    _____ premarital sex
    _____ racial discrimination
    _____ sexual discrimination
    _____ the death penalty
    _____ abortion
    _____ environmental pollution
    _____ teen pregnancy
    _____ criminal violence
    _____ genetic engineering
    _____ illegal drug use (including marijuana)
    _____ same sex marriage
    _____ destruction of wilderness areas/deforestation
    _____ religious fanaticism
    _____ illegal immigration
    _____ poverty/economic inequality
    _____ animal cruelty

2. Which of these moral issues do you consider to be the most serious one confronting human beings today?

3. What is it that makes this issue so morally significant for you?

4. Is there any other moral issue that is extremely important to you that isn't on this list? What is it about this issue that makes it so important to you?

Sources and Further Reading

Aristotle. *Nicomachean Ethics*. Trans. Martin Ostwald. Englewood Cliffs, NJ: Prentice Hall, 1962.

Eberly, Don E. *The Content of America's Character*. Lanham, MD: Madison Books, 1995.

Liszka, James Jakob. *Moral Competence: An Integrated Approach to the Study of Ethics*. Upper Saddle River, NJ: Prentice-Hall, 1999.

PART ONE

WHAT IS ETHICS ANYWAY?

1

FIRST THINGS FIRST

Case Study: A Case of Revenge

On a Saturday afternoon in April, Billy Slotnik, an eighteen-year-old college freshman, goes with his friend Arnie to the mall to pick up some new Ipod speakers. On this particular Saturday, the mall is very crowded and Billy has been forced to drive around in his 2004 green Honda Civic for some time in order to find a parking space. Eventually he gets lucky and spies an elderly woman leaving a space very close to the entrance of the mall. After waiting patiently several more minutes until this woman leaves her spot, Billy gets ready to park there only to discover that a guy in an expensive, large, black SUV has cut him off and has pulled into the spot that Billy was waiting to occupy.

When Billy confronts this man about his behavior, he dismisses Billy with some disparaging comments and tells him to go $%&# off. He then walks into the mall, leaving Billy seething with rage. Wanting to teach this guy a lesson, Billy tells his friend Arnie that he is going to deface the man's car. Arnie has serious reservations about what Billy is planning to do, but decides that he doesn't want to get involved and says nothing. Billy then takes out his house key, makes a long, deep scratch along the entire left side of the SUV, and takes off feeling vindicated.

Unfortunately for Billy, someone had witnessed the entire incident and was able to provide the police with the color and model of Billy's car as well as the first three digits of his license plate number.

A few days later the police show up at Billy's house, having tracked him down through the partial license plate number that was provided to them. Not wanting to pay to repair the damage he caused or get a police record, Billy lies and says that he was home the whole day on Saturday and had nothing to do with the damaged car. Although Billy's parents know that he was at the mall that day, they decide to back their son up and support his story, since they don't want him to get in any trouble with the police.

Without any hard evidence and with Billy's parents supporting his alibi, the police have no option but to drop the case. As they walk out of the house, one of the policemen, Officer Murphy, confides to his colleague that he is sorry that they didn't have enough evidence to nail Billy, since he really dislikes Eastern Europeans. He goes on to make some ethnic jokes about Eastern Europeans, which his partner laughs at, even though he is a bit uncomfortable with Murphy's overt bigotry.

For Discussion

How would you characterize the behavior of the SUV owner, Billy, Arnie, Billy's parents, Officer Murphy and Murphy's partner? If you were present during any of the incidents in question, what would your advice be to these individuals?

Do the actions of the individuals in question seem to fit into the scope of ethics as you understand it (are these really moral or ethical issues)? Why or why not?

In academic circles ethics is considered to be a major subdivision of the field of philosophy. The term philosophy, derived from the Greek words *philia* (love) and *sophia* (wisdom), literally means the love of wisdom. Philosophy is that field of study that explores the meaning of human existence. Philosophy begins in wonder and asks questions about our place in the cosmos, questions like, "What is the purpose of life?" "Why are we here?" "Where are we ultimately going?" Sometimes these questions can lead to answers that help to make our lives more meaningful; at other times, it is enough simply to raise important philosophical questions, even if the answers to these questions remain somewhat obscure or contentious.

As a discipline, philosophy is usually divided into four main areas: metaphysics (the study of the nature of reality), epistemology (the study of human knowledge), aesthetics (the study of beauty), and, finally, ethics.

The word ethics itself comes from the Greek word *ethos*, meaning custom. The Latin equivalent of this term is *mores* (customs), from which we derive our words moral and morality. Although for our purposes we can use the terms ethics and morality interchangeably, there are those philosophers who argue that the two terms have slightly different meanings. In general, morality usually refers to specific moral codes that different communities or societies impose upon their members to prevent harm to others or to promote group cohesion. The Amish, for example, have their own very unique moral code and this code would be dramatically different from that of, let's say, conservative Jews or Western European liberals. The moral codes of different groups or cultures typically develop over long periods of time, and rarely are subject to intellectual scrutiny or critical examination.

Ethics, on the other hand, begins with an attitude of skepticism. It examines all moral views, including those that are perceived as sacrosanct, with a critical eye. This critical reflection on the truth or validity of moral positions is the hallmark of all legitimate ethical inquiry.

The scope of ethics is vast, indeed. As it is commonly understood, ethics addresses questions about how we ought to live our lives, what the nature of the good life is, and what is the proper way to interact with our fellow human beings (and perhaps with non-humans as well). Needless to say, there is very little in the realm of human activity that is not included somehow in the scope of ethics.

Since it is important to define fields of study as precisely as possible at the onset of any intellectual journal, our definition of will have to be broad enough to encompass the vast scope of ethical inquiry, while at the same time maintaining the focus on skepticism as the hallmark of this endeavor. For our purposes, then, we can define ethics simply as *the critical and rational examination of questions of right and wrong in human action.*

The Origin of Ethics

Although human beings have probably engaged in some form of moral reflection since the beginning of time, the formal study of ethics probably began with the ancient Greeks, who made a conscious effort to apply logic and reason to the study of moral questions. One of the first people to systematically begin to inquire about the right way to live was a fellow named Socrates, who lived in the fifth century before Christ in Athens. Socrates was the son of Sophronicus, a sculptor, and Phaenarete, a midwife. During the early part of his life, he seems to have followed in his father's footsteps, working as a sculptor. When he was a young man, however, Socrates turned his attention to Philosophy, and soon devoted himself almost exclusively to studying questions of ethics. He came to believe that it was his mission to act as a kind of "gadfly" to the Athenian people, provoking them into recognizing their moral ignorance. Socrates' goal in interrogating his fellow citizens was not simply to drive them crazy (although he probably unintentionally succeeded in doing this as well). Through the act of moral questioning, he hoped to find some objective standard right and wrong that would aid human beings in determining the right way to live their lives.

Needless to say, his constant interrogation did not endear him to all the citizens of Athens. While Socrates developed a following among many of the more idealistic young men of Athens, he soon incurred the wrath of some of the most powerful men in the city. In 399 B.C. Socrates was put on trial for atheism (not believing in the gods of Athens) and corrupting the youth of the city (by teaching them to question everything). In the end, the jury found Socrates guilty as charged and condemned him to death by the drinking of hemlock.

Socrates' goal of trying to discover some objective criteria for determining right and wrong was taken up by his equally famous disciple, Plato. In his dialogues, in which the character of Socrates plays a central role, and in his great work, The Republic, Plato attempted to ground moral behavior in some transcendent Good that is absolute, eternal and unchanging. Plato's own student, Aristotle, took a decidedly different turn from his master, rejecting Plato's otherworldly approach to ethics. Instead, his approach focused on goods—or virtues—that are extremely practical and down-to-earth. The differences between these two giants of ancient philosophy can be noted in Raphael's famous painting, "The School of Athens." Plato, on the left, is portrayed as pointing upward towards the transcendent realm; Aristotle, on the right, is stretching out his hand horizontally, clearly indicating his comfort with this world of change and impermanence.

Since ancient times, scores of philosophers in various countries have struggled to find the basic principles of moral living. Like Plato and Aristotle, many of these philosophers came up with radically different, and sometimes even opposing, moral principles. Throughout this text, we will examine the ideas of many of these great philosophers and attempt to assess how successful they were in finding an objective basis for moral action.

Divisions of Ethics

There are two traditional subdivisions in ethics:

Non-Normative Ethics is descriptive or empirical. This form of ethics does not attempt to tell us how we ought to behave, but rather simply describes how people typically behave. Anthropologists, psychologists, and sociologists, for example, also study human behavior. The anthropologist might examine certain customs among members of an East African tribe; a sociologist, the group dynamics of certain inner city gang members, the psychologist, the behavior of individuals diagnosed with a specific psychological disorder. They would study all of these forms of behavior, however, without any reference to the rightness or wrongness of the actions in question.

Let's take a rather extreme example: Certain tribes in East Africa engage in what is known as female circumcision (also known as genital mutilation). Using a blade or some kind of sharp device—occasionally even shards of glass have been known to be used—the genitalia of unmarried girls are mutilated with the result that sexual intercourse is extremely painful for these young women after they are married. This serves a dual purpose: first, because the vaginal opening is now smaller, husbands derive greater pleasure from the sexual act, and, second, the girls are less likely to engage in adultery, because the sex act is so unpleasant for them.

Now an anthropologist would certainly study this practice, attempting to understand the origins of the custom and the rationale behind it. What an anthropologist would not do, however, is pass a value judgment upon the actions being performed. His job is simply to describe the behavior and attempt to explain it. That's why non-normative is described as descriptive in nature.

Normative Ethics, on the other hand, is prescriptive rather than descriptive. Take the example of female circumcision once again. The ethicist studying this action might very well start from the same place as the anthropologist. She would want to understand the action completely—its origins, history, rationale, etc.—but the ethicist would go one step further than the anthropologist by evaluating the moral status of the act in question and attempting to justify the rightness or wrongness of the act by referring to clear, consistent, rational principles. In this specific case, almost all ethicists would argue that female circumcision is morally wrong, although they might base their judgment on widely divergent principles (respect for the individual, human rights, the effects that this tradition has on the common good of the societies in which it is performed, etc.).

As you can see from this example, normative ethics attempts to tell us how human beings ought to behave. Normative ethics also provides guidelines and norms that can be used in real life situations when one is confronted with moral dilemmas. This is the form of ethics that we will focus on in this text.

Normative Ethics in turn can be broken down again into two major divisions.

General Normative Ethics is the study of the general principles that determine rightness or wrongness in human conduct. This area of ethics answers the question of how one ought to behave in all circumstances.

Although there are numerous principles that can be studied in the field of normative ethics, most ethicists focus on a few main ones that have stood the test of time: ethical egoism, utilitarianism, deontology, rights theory, and virtue ethics. In principle, almost any moral question can be resolved by referring to one or more of these theories. Furthermore, after studying these main theories for some time, most people find that their own moral position fits quite nicely into one or more of these great ethical traditions. Since this text focuses mainly on general normative ethics, these are the theories that we will eventually be examining in the second part of this book.

Applied Normative Ethics takes general principles of rightness and wrongness in human conduct and applies them to specific areas or realms of reality. Areas of applied ethics include business ethics, environmental ethics, medical ethics, communication ethics, and sexual ethics. Basically just about any domain of human activity could be examined through the lens of applied ethics. A course in environmental ethics, for example, might examine moral issues related to animals—factory farming, animal experimentation, hunting, etc.—by applying theories like those we will be studying in this text to these sorts of specific issues.

Although this text focuses on general normative ethics, we will certainly be using examples from several different areas of applied normative ethics to help elucidate the theories we are discussing. For the most part, however, the cases studies and exercises that are included in this text come from an area of applied ethics that is sometimes referred to as "everyday ethics." In everyday ethics, we apply the great moral theories to the kinds of moral questions you will inevitably struggle with throughout your life—for example, whether to lie to a sick family member, have sexual relations on a first date, or betray the trust of a friend.

Now that we know how ethics fits into the general scheme of philosophy, there are just a few more terms we need to deal with before we can begin to explore the field of ethics in greater depth.

Getting Our Terms Straight

When the average person makes moral statements or judgments, they usually use certain terms interchangeably. For most people the terms *moral, right,* and *good* all refer to behavior that is judged to be acceptable or correct from their perspective, while *immoral, wrong* or *bad* refers to behavior that is judged to be unacceptable or incorrect. Although these terms carry more nuances than the person on the street may be aware of, for our purposes we can also use them interchangeably.

Quite often moral terms are used not only to describe behavior or action, but also to describe a person's character. Thus when we refer to someone as being a *moral person* we are making a judgment that his character is good or virtuous; conversely, when we refer to someone as being an *immoral person* we are claiming that his character is bad, wicked or evil. We should be very careful, however, when we label individuals, rather than their actions, as moral or immoral, good or bad, since we often lack enough information about an individual's character or motivations to make these judgments properly. It might be easy enough to make a moral judgment about Hitler's character, but it is a bit more difficult to do so in the case of, let's say, Richard Nixon.

There are two other terms that are often used in ethical discourse that should be kept in mind.

The term *amoral* means having no sense of right or wrong. Babies, small children, severely mentally handicapped individuals and sociopaths can be said to be amoral and, as such, are usually not deemed to be morally responsible for their actions. The word *non-moral* means outside the realm of morality. Fields of study, such as genetics and physics, or inanimate objects, such as guns or nuclear weapons are essentially non-moral. The old cliché, "Guns don't kill people, people do," therefore, is correct because guns themselves are neither moral nor immoral.

For Further Discussion

Which of the following individuals would you describe as behaving immorally? Be prepared to explain what it is about these acts that you believe to be immoral:

1. A 27-year-old man who has no ambition in life, who still lives in his parent's house, and who is content to hang out and smoke pot every day rather than trying to be a "productive" member of

the community.

2. A 17-year-old high school junior who frequently gossips and reveals information told to her in confidence.

3. A 20-year-old college junior who thinks that women are simply objects to be used for his pleasure.

4. A 25-year-old woman who accidentally gets pregnant after casual sex and opts to have an abortion because she feels that having a baby will prevent her from advancing in her career as a corporate lawyer.

5. A 30-year-old man who believes that all minorities are inferior but who doesn't act upon his racist tendencies.

6. A wealthy, attractive, and stylish 35-year-old woman who never says "thank you" or "please."

7. A middle-class mother of four who believes that her only moral obligation is to her family and does nothing to help those in need in the larger community.

8. A 40-year-old man who regularly eats chicken and hamburgers.

9. An affluent 60-year-old woman who owns several expensive fur coats and wears them regularly during the winter.

10. A teenager who carves the name of his girlfriend in the trunk of a tree so deep in a forest that no one will ever notice it.

Further Reading

At one point or another, as you read this text, you may become interested in finding out more information about some of the ethicists described in this book or delving a bit more deeply into their ideas. If so, the following works are highly recommended:

Ashby, Warren. *A Comprehensive History of Western Ethics: What Do We Believe?* Amherst, NY: Prometheus Books, 1997.

Becker, Lawrence and Charlotte. *A History of Western Ethics.* Hamden, CT: Garland, 1991.

Bourke, Vernon. *A History of Ethics.* Garden City, NY: Doubleday, 1968.

Fieser, James. *Moral Philosophy Through the Ages.* Mountain View, CA: Mayfield Publishing Company, 2001.

MacIntyre, Alasdair. *A Short History of Ethic*s. New York: Macmillan, 1998.

Schneewind, J.B., ed. *Moral Philosophy from Montaigne to Kant.* 2 Vols. Cambridge: Cambridge University Press, 1990.

Wagner, Michael. *An Historical Introduction to Moral Philosophy.* Englewood Cliffs, NJ: Prentice Hall, 1990.

chapter 2

WHAT IS A MORAL ACT?

Case Study: Under the Influence

Johnny Santaniello was born into a poor family on Chicago's South Side. His father, who worked in construction, had a serious alcohol problem that led to his being fired from numerous jobs and eventually dying from liver cancer when Johnny was only 11. Johnny was raised by his mother, who was not able to provide him with much guidance or supervision, because she was working so many hours to support the family.

The neighborhood that Johnny grew up in was rough by any standards. Most of Johnny's friends were heavy drug users by the time they became teenagers and many spent considerable time in juvenile facilities, which only served to fuel their addictions to drugs. Although Johnny always tried to avoid using hard drugs, to fit in with his friends he would occasionally smoke pot. Unlike his friends, however, Johnny was eventually planning to go to college, anticipating that his decent performance as a varsity lacrosse player would get him an athletic scholarship at one of the colleges in his area.

During his senior year of high school, however, Johnny had a string of bad luck that pushed him over the edge. During a lacrosse game, he seriously damaged his knee, effectively ending his career as a lacrosse player. At the same time, Johnny's girlfriend of six years broke up with him because she became interested in another guy. The combination of these two events pushed Johnny into a state of depression and, to forget his problems, he began to abuse alcohol and assorted prescription drugs.

One night, when Johnny was driving home high from a combination of alcohol, pot, and pills, he accidentally drove over the dividing line on the road and crashed into a car occupied by an elderly couple. Although Johnny survived the crash, both occupants of the other car were killed. Johnny was arrested shortly after the accident.

During his trial, Johnny's attorney tried to plead that his client could not be held responsible for the accident because he was not fully in control of his actions due to his drug addiction. He also pleaded for leniency because of the hard life that Johnny had led. The prosecutor argued that Johnny deserved significant prison time because he was responsible for developing his addiction and freely chose to drive a car when he knew that he would be getting high.

For Discussion

Do you think that Johnny is morally responsible for killing the elderly couple, or do you think that the specific circumstances of his life diminish, or even completely remove, his moral culpability? If you were a member of the jury selected to decide Johnny's fate, who would you side with: Johnny's defense lawyer or the prosecutor?

Voluntary and Involuntary Acts

On a daily basis, human beings perform a multitude of different acts. Some of these are fairly unimportant—deciding, for example, what clothes you will wear today or what you will have for dessert. Others may be incredibly significant—for instance, deciding whether you should seek out revenge for some insult or whether you should cheat on your income tax.

All of the acts we perform no matter how insignificant or monumental can be divided into two kinds: voluntary acts or involuntary acts. Voluntary acts are those acts we perform knowingly (i.e., consciously) and freely (i.e., with consent of the will), and for which we, therefore, are responsible. Voluntary acts can be further divided into two additional types: perfect voluntary acts or imperfect voluntary acts. A perfect voluntary act is one that is performed with full knowledge and full freedom. An imperfect voluntary act is one in which knowledge and/or freedom is either not full or lacking in some way.

Involuntary acts, on the other hand, are those performed either without knowledge or without freedom, and for which we cannot be held responsible. When a person commits an act without any foreknowledge or out of some necessity, we rarely, if ever, hold that person morally responsible for his acts, just as we would not hold a rock responsible when it falls through the force of its own weight onto someone's head.

As we continue on with this chapter and with the rest of this text, it will be extremely important to keep in mind the following principle: for an act to be moral in the true sense of the word, it must be a voluntary act. If an act is performed either without knowledge *or* without freedom, it usually is not considered within the realm of morality, since moral actions must involve some degree of conscious choice and deliberation. As we shall see, there are many factors that can affect the knowledge we possess and the freedom that we have to act in a particular situation.

Factors Affecting Knowledge

In general, a person is not considered responsible for acts done in ignorance. There are two kinds of ignorance: invincible ignorance and vincible ignorance. *Invincible ignorance* is ignorance that cannot be removed through effort or diligence. Because invincible ignorance destroys voluntariness, it also removes all responsibility from a person for the acts he performs. Imagine, for example, that a hunter in a remote part of the forest where there usually are no human beings sees something moving in the brush and believes it to be a deer. Only upon firing does he realize that he has killed another hunter, who chose not to wear the required orange safety vest that would have identified him to others. Such an individual would probably not be convicted of manslaughter, because he had no way of knowing that it was a human being in the brush.

Vincible ignorance, on the other hand, is ignorance that could have been removed through effort or greater diligence. Because it involves some degree of choice, it may lessen but does not free us from responsibility. Take, for example, the parents of a teenager, who have a sneaking suspicion that their son is having parties with his friends involving alcohol, but who prefer not to know too much about what is going on. In general, these parents would be responsible for the actions their child performs, because they had the ability to dispel their ignorance, but chose not to do so.

Factors Affecting Freedom

It is also a general principle of moral philosophy that a person can only be held responsible for actions committed freely. Whatever a person does out of necessity—whatever he cannot help doing—he is not responsible for. There are several factors that can affect human freedom:

Concupiscence has traditionally been defined as a movement of strong passion produced by the apprehension of some good or evil. The passions are love and hatred, desire and aversion, joy and sadness, hope and despair, courage and fear, and anger. These passions are neither good nor evil in and of themselves. They can be used by human beings for the purpose of self-preservation and great acts of compassion, but they can become evil if they are not regulated by reason.

Concupiscence can take either of two forms. In the case of antecedent concupiscence, a passion sweeps over a person without his intending it. Antecedent passion lessens freedom, and, in some cases may even remove it completely, because it hinders the reflection of reason. The classic example of antecedent concupiscence is the case of the wife who walks in on her husband in bed with another woman, and in a fit of rage kills them both. In such cases, many juries find defendants innocent by reason of temporary insanity caused by the influence of intense passion.

In general, the more intensive antecedent concupiscence is, the more it affects human freedom. However, unless concupiscence is so violent as to deprive one temporarily of the use of reason, it does not completely eliminate the power to refuse consent. When the will does consent, therefore, to the performance of wrongful acts, even though this consent may be reluctant, there is still freedom of choice and therefore responsibility for the act.

Another form of concupiscence is known as consequent concupiscence, in which strong emotions are freely admitted, consented to, or deliberately aroused, and therefore are completely voluntary. The best illustration of this sort of concupiscence would be the person who fuels her rage over some personal insult and then lashes out at the perpetrator later on. Since the anger in this case is deliberately aroused, this individual is said to be acting with full freedom of the will, and, therefore, is fully responsible for her actions.

Fear is a movement of passion formed by a threatened evil difficult to avoid. Fear can certainly affect freedom of the will to some degree. In the case of acts performed out of great fear, such fear can at times lessen, though not completely remove, responsibility, since human freedom is not destroyed completely. The only exception to this principle would be in the case of grave fear caused by the perception of some extreme evil, which one cannot easily avoid. In the standard plot of many action films, for example, a child is kidnapped and his parents are asked to perform a criminal activity in order to prevent their child from being killed. In an extreme situation like this one, one would have to acknowledge that the parents' extreme fear for their child's safety might very well exculpate them for certain immoral acts which they may have felt compelled to perform.

Coercion is usually defined as force, which compels a person to do something contrary to his will, brought to bear by some extrinsic agent. When someone is forced to perform an action which they otherwise wouldn't be inclined to do, we say that the person is being compelled to act through coercive means. If the coercion is irresistible, then an individual is not responsible for any acts that he may be compelled to perform. The caveat here is that to demonstrate that one was forced to act through coercive means, one must also demonstrate that he at least attempted some resistance. In some cases—for example, date rape—where a person is unable to offer any external resistance, internal resistance alone is usually considered adequate to eliminate responsibility.

In 1974 Patty Hearst, a wealthy heiress, was kidnapped from her Berkeley, California apartment by members of the Symbionese Liberation Army, a terrorist organization. Photographed wielding an assault rifle while robbing a bank, Hearst was later arrested in a San Francisco apartment with other SLA members. There were those at the time who claimed that Hearst was a willing participant in the criminal acts that she performed, and therefore, should be held responsible for them. Her attorney, F. Lee Bailey, argued that Hearst was compelled to act because of fear that her captors would kill her, and that her fear of death was so overwhelming that she was effectively brainwashed into acting as she did. Patty Hearst was eventually convicted of bank robbery and was sentenced to seven years in prison. Her sentence was eventually commuted by President Jimmy Carter and she served only 22 months in prison before she was released. To this day no one really knows for sure whether Hearst was truly coerced into joining the illegal activities of a terrorist organization or whether she was, to one degree or another, a consenting participant.

Habit is a readiness, borne of repeated acts, for doing certain things. If you perform certain acts long enough (e.g., smoking, drinking alcohol, etc.), these acts to a certain extent take on the form of necessity (i.e., you have a difficult time not doing them). It would seem at first glance that habit would eliminate responsibility, since acts done through habit appear almost involuntary. Deliberately admitted habits (e.g., smoking), however, are considered voluntary at least in their causes (e.g., the free choice to smoke that first cigarette) if not completely in their effects. In general, opposed habit lessens voluntariness, and sometimes precludes it completely.

Are We Really Free?

For an act to be a moral act in the true sense of the term, it must be performed voluntarily. This assumes that human beings are capable of acting freely. But is this necessarily the case?

As far back as ancient times, some philosophers came to question whether it is even possible to perform an act with complete freedom of the will. These philosophers, known as Determinists, argued that human beings are compelled by various factors—referred to as antecedent causes—to act in certain predetermined ways, and that, therefore, true freedom of the will is an illusion. The determinist argument is usually summarized in the following way:

> P1: An action is free only if a person could have chosen to do other than he did.
> P2: But all actions are determined by preceeding events (antecedent causes).
> C: Therefore, no action is free.

Determinist theory can take various forms. Biological determinists argue that basic human biology and our specific genetic make-ups determine what kinds of people we will ultimately become and even what kinds of actions we will perform. Biological determinists, for example, argue that things like sexual orientation are predetermined by our biological make-up. It makes no sense then to argue that gay men or women have some kind of choice in the matter or that they can "convert" if they make up their minds to.

Another common form of determinist theory is known as psychological determinism, which posits that deep-rooted psychic forces explain most of human behavior. Sigmund Freud, the father of psychoanalytic theory, in particular believed that human beings are determined by unconscious drives (e.g., the Oedipal complex) that society forces them to repress. He completely rejects the idea that simply because we feel that we are free that we actually are:

> As is known, many persons argue against the assumption of an absolute psychic determinism by referring to an intense feeling

of conviction that there is a free will. The feeling of conviction exists, but it is not incompatible with the belief in determinism. Like all normal feelings, it must be justified by something. But, so far as I can observe, it does not manifest itself in weighty and important decisions; on these occasions, one has much more the feeling of psychic compulsion and gladly falls back on it....

On the other hand, it is in trivial and indifferent decisions that one feels sure that he could just as easily have acted differently, that he acted of his own free will, and without any motives. From our analyses we therefore need not contest the right of the feeling of conviction that there is a free will (161-162).

Thus for Freud all of our significant decisions are determined by unconscious motives. Only the most trivial decisions—and what they are he does not explain—are free of such psychic conditioning.

Finally behaviorism is another psychological theory that argues that human behavior was determined not by unconscious drives, but rather by environmental factors. The most prominent of these behaviorist was B.F. Skinner, who in his works *Beyond Freedom and Dignity* and *Walden II*, argued that human beings are "conditioned" to act in specific ways by their environment, and that freedom, therefore, is an illusion. The only way to change a person's behavior according to Skinner is to change his environment. Skinner recommended the use of positive and negative reinforcement to alter human behavior, and believed that a perfect society could be created simply by figuring out how to condition people properly.

Responding to Determinism

In attempting to respond to the challenge of determinism, those who hold a belief in the existence of freedom of the will often begin by acknowledging that certain external factors can indeed affect human freedom. However, they dispute the fact that human beings have absolutely no freedom of decision-making. These theorists pose a number of objections to determinist theory:

Awareness of our personal freedom. As human agents our basic assumption is that the acts we perform are done freely, consciously, and deliberately. When you go to the mall to buy a pair of boots, for example, you don't think to yourself, "I have no choice in which pair of boots I buy." You automatically assume that you yourself decide what to buy, not some unconscious drives or behavior conditioning. The very act of weighing the pros and cons before we act demonstrates that, at least in our own minds, we assume that we are free. As Corliss Lamont puts it:

> There is an unmistakable intuition of virtually every human being that he is free to make the choices he does and that the deliberations leading to those choices are also free flowing. The normal man feels too, after he has made a decision, that he could have decided differently. That is why regret or remorse for a past choice can be so disturbing (3).

Assumption of Moral Responsibility. In our society we frequently bestow praise on those who perform worthy or noble actions (e.g., the fireman who saves a child from a burning building) and assign blame to those who violate legal or moral norms (i.e., the neighbor who mows his lawn at 7am on a Saturday). But if no one does anything freely, then they are not responsible for their actions and neither deserving of praise nor blame.

Punishment of the Guilty. We believe that people who break the law should receive punishment for their crimes. But, if people are not free when they commit criminal activities, then they should not be punished for their actions. Drug dealers and rapists would undoubtedly appreciate this line of argumentation.

Controlling Desires. Psychological determinists argue that human beings are the victims of desires that they cannot control. And yet there are numerous instances of individuals who have overcome their deep-rooted desires and addictions through the force of their wills. They are capable, in other words, of overcoming their conditioning, which implies some degree of freedom.

The ultimate problem with determinism is that it ultimately renders morality impossible since, as we have already seen, freedom of the will is an essential characteristic of moral action. If you eliminate freedom, therefore, you eliminate morality (as most of us understand it, anyway). For this very reason most moral thinkers accept the existence of at least limited freedom of the will.

Certainly no one would argue that human behavior is not affected by various factors—aberrant mental states, the environment, our genetic makeup, etc. The question is whether these factors determine our behavior. Indeterminists—those who accept the existence of freedom of the will—believe that this is not the case. They argue that there is a fundamental difference between human beings and all other things in the natural world. Unlike all other entities, human beings are conscious of the operation of the natural and psychological laws that affect them. We can step back and reflect on these laws as more or less objective observers, and make our choices in light of these reflections. We are capable, in other words, of choosing to give in to our conditioning or not.

Take two people, for example, Willard and Mordecai. Willard grew up in a warm and loving household, with parents who took very good care of him, and who provided him with ample opportunities for personal and intellectual growth. Mordecai, on the other hand, grow up in a poor, abusive household in a neighborhood rampant with drugs and violent crime. All of us would agree that, given his background, Mordecai would have a much more difficult time than Willard in becoming a productive and responsible member of the society. But both these individuals ultimately have to choose how they are going to behave. Certainly it would take much more effort for Mordecai to resist the temptations to give in to drug use and criminal activity than it would for Willard. We would have to argue, however, that although it may be much harder for Mordecai to remain on the "straight and narrow" path, it is certainly not impossible. For an indeterminist the ability to break free of our conditioning is the "proof" that human beings are in fact free.

The determinist would argue that this belief in human freedom is simply an illusion—a pipe dream that we create in order to avoid the unpleasant fact that our actions are as determined as those of any other natural object in the universe. In the end, we have no way of knowing with utter certitude whether we are indeed free or not. The arguments of the determinist and the indeterminist are equally inconclusive. The moral enterprise, however, demands that we at least assume we are free, until it can be proven otherwise.

For Further Discussion

You are a representative on a college disciplinary tribunal set up to determine how students who have committed violations of school conduct codes should be punished. The following students have all argued that they are not responsible for the actions they committed for the reasons specified. Your job is to determine the degree of responsibility that each student has for the acts they committed and what sort of punishment, if any, would be most applicable:

- A sophomore from a financially strapped family steals $50 out of a wealthy student's dorm room. He maintains that he was driven to commit this action because he didn't have enough money to pay for the books he needed for class.

- In a heated exchange an African American student is called a racial slur by another student. In a fit of rage, he retaliates by hitting the student. He later claims that his anger over the insult drove him to respond in violence and that he shouldn't be held responsible for his actions.

- A freshman with a history of psychological problems is caught surreptitiously taking pictures with his cell phone of girls' bare feet as they sunbathe on the campus green. He claims that he has a foot fetish and can't control himself.

- A wealthy student is caught stealing a $1 folder from the campus bookstore. He maintains that he is being treated for kleptomania and was unable to stop himself from stealing. He also says that he never steals anything worth more than $2.

- Two students go on a date and when they return to campus begin to engage in consensual intimacies involving kissing and heavy petting. When the female student begins to feel uncomfortable and tells her partner that she wants to stop, he refuses. She reports him to the campus police, but he maintains that she was to blame for willingly arousing him to a point beyond which he could reasonably be expected to control himself.

- A senior goes out drinking with his fraternity buddies during graduation week and becomes extremely drunk. He arrives at his dorm room at 2am, but finds that he has been locked out. Unable to get anyone to open the door for him, he breaks a window to get in. When he is caught by the campus police, he maintains that he was too drunk to know what he was doing, and therefore was not responsible. This is the only time that he has gotten into trouble during his four years at college.

Sources and Further Reading

Double, Richard. *The Non-Reality of Free Will.* New York: Oxford University Press, 1991.

Dworkin, Gerald. *The Theory and Practice of Autonomy.* Cambridge: Cambridge University Press, 1988.

Ekstrom, Laura Waddell. *Agency and Responsibility*. Boulder, CO: Westview Press, 2001.

Freud, Sigmund. *Psychopathology of Everyday Life*. New York: Modern Library, 1966.

Kane, Robert. *Free Will and Values*. Albany, NY: SUNY Press, 1985.

Lamont, Corliss. *Freedom of Choice Affirmed*. New York: Horizon, 1967.

Skinner, B.F. *Beyond Freedom and Dignity*. New York: Alfred A. Knopf, 1971.

—. *Walden II*. New York: Macmillan, 1976.

Watson, Gary. *Free Will*. Oxford: Oxford University Press, 1982.

Wolf, Susan. *Freedom Within Reason*. New York: Oxford University Press, 1990.

3

CHALLENGES TO ETHICAL THEORY

Case Study: Lucy and Elsie

Lucy Cappamezzo is a 35-year-old assistant vice-president at Chase Manhattan Bank. Since she graduated from college thirteen years ago, she has worked hard to move her way up the corporate ladder. She was particularly excited about becoming an executive at a prestigious organization like Chase, because there are not many women in this kind of upper level position. Her life right now is exactly what she wants it to be: she commands an extremely high salary. She owns a wonderful condo on the upper East Side of Manhattan facing the river, and she has been told that she has the potential to move to the top of her organization.

A few months ago Lucy met Brad Sullivan, a 37-year-old business-man, whose computer software company has really started to take off, generating millions of dollars each year. Brad is currently separated from his wife of five years and has a four-year-old daughter who he visits on occasion. From the moment that Brad and Lucy met at a local East Side bar, they were immediately attracted to one another, and started dating regularly. Neither of them, however, can afford to take time out of their busy schedules to make any kind of real commitment to a part-ner, but both would like to have a casual, noncommittal, sexual relation-ship. They meet about three times a week for dinner, companionship, and sexual intercourse.

When Lucy's mother Elsie Cappamezzo found out about this arrange-ment she became extremely agitated and told her daughter that her behavior was completely unacceptable. She said that there were rules about how people should behave sexually, and that Lucy was breaking all of them. Quoting both the Old and the New Testament as well as some recent pronouncements of the Pope, Elsie maintained that Lucy was putting her immortal soul in danger through her immoral and inde-cent behavior.

In reply, Lucy told her mother that the rules that she was talking about simply reflect her own opinions about sexual matters. Each person, Lucy said, has his or her own ideas about right and wrong, and that hers were just different (not any worse) than her mother's. In the end, Lucy told her mother, all a person can do in life is try to be faithful to her own heart, and follow it wherever it may lead.

The discussion quickly degenerated into a full-blown argument, with Lucy remaining firm in her belief that lifestyle choices like hers were simply matters of preference and her mother arguing that God has ex-pressly forbidden the sort of behavior in which Lucy was currently en-gaged. Because neither party could understand the other's position and because neither was willing to listen to views that contradicted her own, the two stormed off angrily, vowing not to speak again until the other started acting more sensibly.

For Discussion

How would you characterize Lucy's and Elsie's approach to moral issues? Which approach makes the most sense to you personally? Why? Do you see any potential problems with either of these approaches to ethics? If so, what?

Before we begin to examine the essential characteristics of moral prin-ciples, it would be useful to take a look at two approaches to ethics that pose enormous challenges to the moral enterprise, because each is so seductive in their simplicity. These theories go by the names of subjec-tivism and dogmatism. Although neither theory holds up upon careful examination, it's fairly easy to fall into the trap of approaching ethics either subjectivistically or dogmatically. As we'll see, the danger with both these approaches is that each in its own unique way undermines the very foundations of ethics as a rational enterprise.

Subjectivism

In order to understand the philosophical roots of subjectivism, one must first recognize that for many modern philosophers scientific statements seem to be of a different sort altogether than moral statements. Let's start with a little experiment to help illustrate this point. Read the two following statements, and ask yourself if they are true or false:

1. Statement #1: "It is raining outside."
2. Statement #2: "The death penalty is morally wrong."

What specific criteria did you use to determine whether each of these statements was true or false? (In other words, how did you determine whether or not it is true that it is raining outside? And how did you determine whether or not it is true that the death penalty is morally wrong?) Do these statements appear to be of the same kind or are they different in some way? Which of these statements seems more objective to you? Why?

If you are like many students, you probably thought that the scientific statement ("It is raining out.") was more objective in nature than the moral statement ("The death penalty is morally wrong."). You may have thought that the second statement was more a matter of personal opinion than objective fact and perhaps less open to being verified as true or false than the first statement. If this sort of response reflects the way that you viewed these two sorts of statements, then, congratulations, you are a subjectivist!

Subjectivists believe that, whereas scientific statements can be judged to be true or false depending on whether or not they correspond with reality, moral statements seem to lack this kind of objective basis. It is clear that a scientific statement like "it is raining out" can be proved or disproved by a careful observation of the way the world operates. Look out the window. If it is, in fact, raining outside, you know that the statement is true; if it is not raining, you know the statement is false. The same is true with more complex sorts of scientific statements as well (e.g., "E=mc²" or the law of gravity).

On the other hand, if I were to maintain that "the death penalty is morally wrong," such a statement would seem to preclude the kind of demonstration that one finds in science. What "proof" could I give that would absolutely convince any rational person that my statement is true?

This apparent difference between scientific and moral statements has led certain philosophers to question whether there is any objective basis for our moral claims. Subjectivists argue that such claims instead simply represent our personal preferences or our individual feelings about certain actions. One of the main proponents of this theory was David

Hume (1711-1776), a British philosopher whose aim was to debunk those thinkers who believed that they could provide a foundation for ethics that is grounded in reason. In Book III of his *Treatise of Human Nature*, Hume presents one of the earliest and most influential defenses of a theory of subjectivism. He begins by arguing that it is the passions, not reason, that moves us to perform certain actions. It is futile, then, to look for a rational basis for our moral acts:

> Take any action allowed to be vicious: willful murder, for instance. Examine it in all lights and see if you can find that matter of fact or real existence, which you can call vice. In whichever way you take it, you find only certain passions, motives, volitions and thoughts. There is no other matter of fact in the case. The vice entirely escapes you, as long as you consider the object. You never can find it, till you turn reflection into your own breast and find a sentiment of disapprobation which arises in you towards this action. Here is a matter of fact; but it is the object of feeling, not of reason. It lies within yourself, not in the object (468).

Thus for Hume our judgments about whether certain actions are right or wrong simply reflect whether one approves or disapproves of the action being performed. Morality in this approach becomes nothing more than a matter of taste, not unlike a preference that one might have for hamburgers over pizza. For example, to say that abortion is wrong is to express nothing more than my distaste for the termination of the life of the fetus. It is simply to say, "I disapprove of this type of behavior." But such a judgment says nothing about the objective status of the act itself. The subjectivist would, in fact, argue that the statement says more about the attitude of the speaker than about the nature of the act being spoken about.

Taken to its logical conclusion, subjectivism inevitably leads to another "ism" that is equally controversial in ethics—relativism. If our moral judgments are simply a matter of preference, and there is no objective basis for determining whether one set of moral preferences are superior to any other, then we must hold that all moral perspectives are equally valid. In the end, if I believe something to be right, then it must be right—at least for me. Nor can our moral preferences be subject to dispute. Just as we wouldn't think of criticizing someone who prefers hamburgers to pizza, we also can't object to those whose lifestyles may seem morally wrong to us. The way a person chooses to live and the specific moral decisions he makes should not ultimately be viewed as better or worse than anyone else's. In the words of the Roman sage: "De gustibus non est disputandum" (Taste must not be disputed).

Believe it or not, many individuals in our society are probably subjectivists without even knowing it. For example, in the course of a heated argument over the death penalty, one of the debaters might throw up his or her hands in disgust, shouting, "Well, you're entitled to your perspective and I'm entitled to mine." Or after a 50 minute Ethics class in which the instructor believes that he has made a persuasive case that partial birth abortion is wrong, systematically refuting opposing arguments and successfully countering all objections, at least one student will inevitably come up with the following kind of retort: "That's just your opinion." Even in those situations where they may personally feel a specific type of behavior is morally repugnant, they feel extremely hesitant to argue that it is objectively wrong, lest they be accused of being moral absolutists. "Who am I to say," such students lament, "how other people ought to behave?"

Despite the popularity of subjectivism as a moral approach, there are some obvious problems with such an approach to ethics:

There are objective wrongs. Certain extreme acts—rape, torture and child abuse—seem to be wrong, not just because of one's personal distaste for them, but because of the immoral nature of the acts themselves. Other less extreme acts—neglect of one's children, disloyalty to one's friends, marital infidelity —also seem objectively wrong to us, but because of the complexity of these issues we might need to spend more time developing cogent arguments to explain exactly why they are wrong.

Real argumentation implies an objective basis for our moral claims. There seems to be something intuitively wrong with subjectivism as well. Although when many people argue for or against some moral position they clearly do so in a way that signifies that they are simply expressing their opinion or preference on the subject, others actually attempt to give some rational justification for their position. The man who argues against the death penalty, for example, by attempting to demonstrate that it does not reduce violent crime or that it is an unjust means of punishing criminals, clearly believes that there is an objective basis to his moral position. He knows that he is not simply expressing his own preference, but is in fact expressing, however partially and imperfectly, some higher truth about the subject. Insofar as he is open to the reasonable opposing arguments of others—willing to allow, that is, their more convincing arguments to change his position on the subject—he is certainly doing something more than simply expressing a feeling about the death penalty.

Subjectivism precludes criticizing repugnant behavior. If moral judgments are mere opinions, similar to a preference for hotdogs or hamburgers, it is extremely difficult to criticize anyone for their moral viewpoints or behavior, no matter how repugnant they might be. The following example will help to illustrate this problem: Ted Bundy, a serial killer who murdered many young women during his infamous killing spree in the 1990s, expressed his feelings about what he did by espousing an almost perfect philosophy of subjectivism. As Bundy himself recounted:

> Then I learned that all moral judgments are 'value judgments,' that all value judgments are subjective, and that none can be proved to be either 'right' or 'wrong.' I even read somewhere that the Chief Justice of the United States had written that the American Constitution expresses nothing more than collective value judgments. Believe it or not, I figured out for myself— what apparently the Chief Justice couldn't figure out for himself—that if the rationality of one value judgment was zero, multiplying it by millions would not make it one whit more rational. Nor is there any 'reason' to obey the law for anyone, like myself, who has the boldness and daring—the strength of character—to throw off its shackles....I discovered that to become truly free, truly unfettered, I had to become truly uninhibited.
>
> And I quickly discovered that the greatest obstacle to my freedom, the greatest block and limitation to it, consists in the insupportable 'value judgment' that I was bound to respect the rights of others. I asked myself, who were these 'others?' Other human beings, with human rights? Why is it more wrong to kill a human animal than any other animal, a pig or a sheep or a steer? Is your life more than a hog's life to a hog? Why should I be willing to sacrifice my pleasure more for the one than for the other? Surely, you would not, in this age of scientific enlightenment, declare that God or nature has marked some pleasures as 'moral' or 'good' and others as 'immoral' or 'bad'?
>
> In any case, let me assure you, my dear young lady, that there is absolutely no comparison between the pleasure that I might take in eating ham and the pleasure I anticipate in raping and murdering you. This is the honest conclusion to which my edu-

cation has led me—after the most conscientious examination of my spontaneous and uninhibited self (Pojman 30).

The problem that those who intentionally or unintentionally espouse a subjectivistic viewpoint face is how on earth is it possible to criticize someone like Ted Bundy if all moral judgments express nothing more than preferences or opinion? If he were consistent, the subjectivist would have to say that Bundy's moral opinions are as valid as anyone else's. Or he would have to drop his own subjectivism in extreme cases—rape, torture, etc—but then he would be inconsistent.

How would you respond to Ted Bundy's "rationale" for why there is basically nothing wrong with the killing spree that he undertook? Do you think that, if you were faced with the challenge of responding to an argument like his, you would resort to the old platitude, "Well, everyone has his own opinion"? Are you starting to feel a bit uncomfortable now about where subjectivist moral views can ultimately lead? Perhaps you can see why many philosophers argue that subjectivism as a moral approach is not only ill considered, but extremely dangerous as well.

If, after reflecting upon these objections, you agree that subjectivistic attitudes towards moral issues are problematic, perhaps you would be willing to take me up on a challenge: make it a point from now on when you are talking about ethical issues to avoid qualifying moral judgments with phrases like "in my opinion" or "I believe." Force yourself to take a stand on ethical issues, to argue your position strongly and persuasively, and to stand by your moral judgment. If in time you are persuaded by facts or arguments to modify or even contradict your prior moral judgment, that's okay too. It means that you are evolving as a moral thinker. Just recognize that the moral judgments you make should be grounded in something more objective than a mere whim or some shallow preference.

Moral Dogmatism

Another very problematic approach to ethics that I would like to examine can be called "dogmatism," for lack of a better name. A dogmatist is someone who is so absolutely convinced of the truth of his or her viewpoint that he or she is unwilling to accept any countervailing viewpoint no matter how reasonable it might be. Although there are many different breeds of dogmatists, most share certain common characteristics:

- Dogmatists are unshakable in their moral outlook. They have a "black and white" view of reality with no shades of gray. They are rarely, if ever, given to doubts, struggles, or uncertainty.
- Dogmatists believe that their view is the only possible right one, and discount those who have contrary views as being in error or even immoral.
- Dogmatists are usually not willing to argue their position rationally with those who disagree. When asked to defend their positions, they typically will cite an authority figure or "sacred" text as providing all the justification they believe is needed.

At first glance, dogmatism might seem to be almost admirable in an age when so many are given to treating ethics as a matter of opinion. Unlike subjectivists, a dogmatist has no problem taking a moral stand. Dogmatists are also often quite good at living up to their own values and defending them forcefully when necessary.

Examples of dogmatism can be found in almost every domain of life. A political dogmatist, for example, might believe that whatever a pundit or politician who shares his political leanings says must be taken as the gospel truth. Whether such an individual's pronouncements are, at times, contradictory or even illogical does not matter in the least to a committed dogmatist. Dogmatists of various stripes can also be found in the fields of science, education, health care, and, not surprisingly, in religion as well.

In fact, one of the oldest approaches to ethics—Divine Command Theory—is also a good example of religious dogmatism. Although this approach to ethics has always had its adherents, in recent years, in the United States especially, more and more Americans seem to resort to some form of this position when discussing complex moral issues.

Divine Command Theory actually refers to a number of related ethical theories. What they all have in common is that they take God's will to be the foundation for ethics. According to this theory, an act is morally good if God wills or commands it and an act is morally bad if he prohibits or condemns it. Thus the statement, "Adultery is wrong," therefore, simply means, "adultery is forbidden by God." No other justification is needed to decide if an act is right or wrong other than God's command or condemnation. For example, an adherent of this position might maintain that homosexual activity is morally wrong because such actions have been condemned by God. He might go so far as to show the specific passages in scripture or the magisterial proclamations that express God's will, but he would probably not go any further than this to make his case. He certainly would have no need to argue his case based upon the impact that homosexual relations might have on the well being of the larger society, for example.

One philosophical difficulty with this position has been raised by an argument known as the *"Euthyphro* Dilemma." The argument is found in Plato's text of the same name and is named after Euthyphro, Socrates' antagonist in the text. In this ancient dialogue, Socrates asks Euthyprho a perplexing question: "Are morally good acts willed by God because they are morally good or are they morally good because they are willed by God?" Either way that Euthyphro answers the question raises its own set of difficulties.

If Euthyphro attempts to argue the first position—that morally good acts are willed by God because they are morally good—then he faces the independence problem. If morally good acts are willed by God because they are morally good, then they are morally good independently of God's willing them. But this basically is a complete repudiation of Divine Command Theory.

If Euthyphro attempts to argue the second position—that morally good acts are good because they are willed by God—then he faces the arbitrariness problem. In this case morality seems to be based upon little more than the whim of God. Consider this hypothetical case: what if God were to command one to perform abhorrent acts such as torturing a non-believer. Would this then make such acts morally correct? We would have to argue, yes. Although one could argue that God has chosen not to command such acts, there is no reason why he could not. Take God's command to Abraham to kill his son Issac, described in Genesis 22, for instance. What if God didn't stop Abraham from sacrificing his son in the end? Would this mean that such an abhorrent act is morally permissible simply because God willed it?

Besides the philosophical critique posed by the *Euthyphro* Dilemma, there are two other more practical problems with Divine Command Theory:

How do we know what God prohibits? In some cases—rape, murder, incest—there would probably be some agreement among believers about what God forbids. In other cases, there may be much more debate. Take, for instance, the case of divorce. Catholics and conservative Protestants would argue that God forbids divorce while more liberal Protestants might argue that he allows it in certain circumstances. We could consult a sacred text like the Bible but we would probably get conflicting views on just about any moral topic that we were examining. One could also use the Bible in order to justify horrendous acts such as genocide or slavery if one was predisposed to do so.

Finally, which sacred text do we consult to discover God's will: The Bible? The Koran? The Book of Mormon? Adherents to different faiths would argue that their sacred text is the revealed word of God and would reject the legitimacy of other sacred texts. So which sacred text do we look to for the answers to our moral questions and, even more important, what means do we use to interpret this text in order to uncover the will of God?

How are you going to convince an atheist? Not everyone believes in God, and so many people will never buy into the basic premise of Divine Command Theory. The problem is that many individuals who support this theory often are trying to persuade others of the merits of their position, especially when it comes to public policy issues. To argue, for example, that gay marriage is wrong because God has condemned homosexual activity would be completely unpersuasive to a non-believer. It probably would also fail to persuade a more rationally oriented believer who may have his or her own religious reasons for supporting gay marriage—for example, because they believe God wants them to practice compassion towards other human beings.

There are very few people who think of themselves as dogmatists, because to do so would imply a kind of rigid, unreflective personality that most people are unwilling to acknowledge in themselves. And yet dogmatists abound in our society. In fact, if you are prone to thinking in black and white terms about moral issues or if you often resort to arguing about issues based upon the teachings of whatever religion you currently practice, you might be a bit of a dogmatist yourself. If you think this might be the case, I'd like to offer you a challenge: try to discuss moral issues without so often appealing to your religious beliefs or to the teachings of religious authority figures. I'm not telling you to abandon either your religious beliefs or the moral convictions that spring out of them. Just try to make your case in a way that those who are outside your religious framework might be able to accept, rather than presuming that your own beliefs are gospel truth and that anyone who challenges them must automatically be wrong.

If you do this, you may just discover that you actually become more persuasive in making moral arguments, because you'll be speaking to others from their perspective rather than your own. And you might even find that your moral perspectives gain a certain amount of depth from taking a vacation from your own dogmatic sensibilities.

Digging Beneath the Surface

On one level subjectivism and dogmatism would seem to represent polar extremes in ethics. The subjectivist doesn't recognize any objective basis for moral claims, and treats such claims purely as matters of opinion or preference; the dogmatist is so absolute in his moral pronouncements that he refuses to recognize that contrary moral positions might have even the slightest validity. Subjectivists value tolerance and openness to diverse moral perspectives; dogmatists value moral certainty above all else and often view tolerance as a gateway to moral vice. There would seem to be very little that these two ethical approaches could possibly have in common.

And yet dogmatists have much more in common with subjectivists than they might care to acknowledge. Underlying the dogmatists claim to objectivity is always the idea that something is right or wrong because God wills it or forbids it. We've seen that conservative Catholics and liberal Protestants read the same Bible to discover the will of God and yet Catholics interpret the Bible in such a way as to prohibit the possibility of divorce or the use of birth control, while liberal Protestants acknowledge no such prohibitions. It's the same Bible that they are both reading, but the way each group chooses to interpret what they regard as God's will is very different.

Upon what basis, then, does the dogmatist choose to accept one interpretation of scripture over another? According to the views of some religious authority? But then we must ask, upon what basis are the views of one authority figure (the Pope, for example) chosen over the views of another (the Dalai Lama, for instance). In the end, we must acknowledge that the dogmatist's basis for his moral claims is just as subjective as any subjectivists.

Neither of these flawed approaches to ethics in the end is able to provide what we really need in a viable moral position—a rational and objective basis for our moral claims. It remains to be seen if another approach to ethics is possible: one that can provide the kind of solid foundation that can guide us as we navigate our way through the moral challenges that we will inevitably face in our daily lives.

For Further Discussion

The following exercises can either be done individually or in groups, with one group developing the pro position, a second developing the the con position, and the third acting as a kind of jury to see which team's arguments were the most persuasive:

1. Gay Marriage: One of the important moral questions currently being raised in our society is whether or not gay couples should have the right to get married and receive the same benefits as heterosexual couples currently do. Far too often when discussing this issue, those for and against gay marriage base their views on opinions, beliefs, or emotions rather than facts or logic.

    •   Pro Position: Develop as many strong, persuasive arguments as you can in support of gay marriage.
    •   Con Position: Develop as many strong, persuasive arguments as you can in opposition to gay marriage.
    •   Evaluation: Based solely upon the strengths of the arguments that you have developed (and trying, as much as possible, to leave out any biases you have about this issue), explain which position seems the most persuasive to you.

2. The Legalization of Marijuana: Another contentious issue in our society is whether or not marijuana should be legalized. Once again there are passionate people on both sides of this issue, who believe that their position is correct, but who also may be swayed more by emotion than by rational arguments.

    •   Pro Position: Develop as many strong, persuasive arguments as you can in support of the legalization of marijuana.
    •   Con Position: Develop as many strong, persuasive arguments as you can in opposition to the legalization of marijuana.
    •   Evaluation: Based solely upon the strengths of the arguments that you have developed (and trying, as much as possible, to leave out any biases you have about this issue), explain which position seems the most persuasive to you.

Sources and Further Reading

Harman, Gilbert and Thompson, Judith Jarvis. *Moral Objectivity*. Oxford: Blackwell, 1996.

Hume, David. *Treatise of Human Nature*. L.A. Selby-Bigge, ed. Oxford: Clarendon Press, 1978.

Nielsen, Kai. *Why Be Moral?* Buffalo, NY: Prometheus, 1989.

Paul, Ellen Frankel. *Objectivism, Subjectivism, and Relativism in Ethics.* Cambridge: Cambridge University Press, 2008.

Pojman. *Ethics: Discovering Right and Wrong.* 5th ed. Belmont, CA: Wadsworth, 2005.

Rescher, Nicholas. *Objectivity: The Obligations of Impersonal Reason.* Notre Dame: Notre Dame University Press, 1977.

Rorty, Richard. *Objectivity, Relativism, and Truth.* Cambridge: Cambridge University Press, 1991.

Westermarch, Edward. *Ethical Relativity.* Patterson, NJ: Littlefield, 1960.

4

GETTING ETHICS RIGHT

Case Study: Thwarting a Terrorist Attack

Authorities in New York City have recently heard through an informer that a group of Islamic militants living in Brooklyn plan to detonate a "dirty bomb" somewhere in New York within the next two days. Although this bomb can fit into a briefcase, it has the potential to kill hundreds of New Yorkers if it is exploded in a crowded building. The informer who reported this to the police is known for being extremely reliable and information he provided in the past has helped law enforcement officials round up a number of high profile terror suspects.

Raiding an apartment in Williamsburg, where one of the suspected terrorists was said to frequent, police arrested one man, Sadam al Baradi and his wife Fatima. The couple's three children were also taken in the raid and placed in foster care until the case could be sorted out. Sadam, a native of Saudia Arabia, continued to proclaim his innocence, although traces of chemicals that could be used to make a bomb similar to the one described were found in his apartment. When confronted with this evidence, Sadam broke down and told police that in previous weeks, his cousin, Hakkim, a known sympathizer of the terrorist group, Islamic Jihad, had been meeting in the apartment with some of his friends during the day when the family was not around. Through hours of intense interrogation, Sadam continued to maintain that he didn't know anything about his cousin's plans or the whereabouts of those whom authorities suspected were plotting the attack.

The FBI counter-terrorism expert in charge of the case, Fred Dobbs, has come to believe that Sadam probably is not directly involved in the plot, but he also suspects that he has not been honest about his knowledge of his cousin's whereabouts. With only one day before the bomb is set to explode, Dobbs is left with a difficult dilemma: does he continue to use only legal means to interrogate Sadam and risk having hundreds of innocent people die, or should he resort to the use of torture on Sadam, and perhaps even his wife, to get them to reveal the information that he believes they might possess. The methods that he is considering are so extreme that they have been condemned by civilized nations around the world.

For Discussion

Pretend that you are a fellow FBI agent, and that Dobbs has come to you to help him decide on how to proceed in this case. You are known for being a highly objective and rational agent, so Dobbs asks you to come up with the strongest possible arguments for and against torturing Sadam and his wife, and then to advise him on what to do.

The Right Way to Do Ethics: Socrates in the *Crito*

Plato's famous dialogue, the *Crito*, opens with Socrates awaiting his execution in a jail in Athens. He is visited by Crito, a wealthy young friend, who tried to convince him that he ought to flee from prison rather than face death. Socrates's friends, Crito reminds him, are more than willing to use their own considerable wealth to bribe the guards who are watching over Socrates and provide the means for him to escape to some other city. If Socrates chooses not to flee, it will look as though his friends were too cheap or cowardly to save him when they could have and Socrates' enemies will take delight in his downfall.

It would have been all too easy for Socrates to take Crito up on his offer and escape to another Greek city. But Socrates was simply not that kind of man. In his reply to Crito, Socrates lays the foundations for his own approach to moral issues, leaving no doubts that he will be persuaded by sound arguments and not by the opinions of those who do not know what they are talking about, even if they happen to be in the majority:

> Dear Crito, your zeal is invaluable, if a right one; but if wrong, the greater the zeal the greater the evil; and therefore we ought to consider whether these things shall be done or not. For I am and always have been one of those natures who must be guided by reason, whatever the reason may be which upon reflection appears

to me to be the best; and now that this fortune has come upon me, I cannot put away the reasons which I have before given: the principles which I have hitherto honored and revered I still honor, and unless we can find other and better principles on the instant, I am certain not to agree with you; no, not even if the power of the multitude could inflict many more imprisonments, confiscations, deaths, frightening us like children with hobgoblin terrors ....

[Instead we should examine] whether I ought or ought not to try to escape without the consent of the Athenians: and if I am clearly right in escaping, then I will make the attempt; but if not, I will abstain. The other considerations which you mention, of money and loss of character, and the duty of educating children, are, I fear, only the doctrines of the multitude, who would be as ready to call people to life, if they were able, as they are to put them to death—and with as little reason. But now, since the argument has thus far prevailed, the only question which remains to be considered is, whether we shall do rightly either in escaping or in suffering others to aid in our escape and paying them in money and thanks, or whether we shall not do rightly; and if the latter, then death or any other calamity which may ensue on my remaining here must not be allowed to enter into the calculation (*Crito*, 46b-c; 48c-d).

In this passage Socrates rejects the idea that we should rely on our emotion to help us determine the correct way to behave, but should rely instead on reason, logic, and argumentation to make decisions. He also clearly believes that opinions of others don't matter at all in this process, but that we must rely on our own innate wisdom to solve moral problems. In short, if Crito wants Socrates to escape from prison he is going to have to persuade him rationally to do so.

To give Crito some idea about how the process of rational argumentation in ethics might work, Socrates devises three clever arguments to support his own contention that it would be wrong for him to escape from prison. We can summarize these arguments in the following way:

One ought never to intentionally cause harm to anyone.
If Socrates escapes from prison, he will cause harm to the state of Athens.
Therefore Socrates ought not to escape from prison.

If one remains in a state when one had the opportunity to leave it,

then one is making an implied promise to obey its laws (and, of course, one ought always to keep one's promises).
If Socrates flees from prison then he is breaking the state's laws.
Therefore Socrates ought not to escape from prison.

One's state is like one's parent or teacher, and one ought to obey one's parent or teacher.
If Socrates flees from prison, then he is disobeying the state—i.e., his parent and teacher.
Therefore Socrates ought not to escape from prison.

In the end, Crito is unable to persuade Socrates using rational arguments, and Socrates, based upon the force of his own arguments, determines that the morally correct course of action would be for him to remain in prison and face certain death. How many people do you know who would choose death rather than be swayed by a bad argument?

Criteria for Viable Ethical Theories

Socrates' approach to moral issues, as has already been noted, laid the foundation for the future development of the field of ethics. In general, the approach to ethics that Socrates advocates in the *Crito* is one that is characterized by five clear criteria:

1. Rationality

Ethics is more than a matter of feeling, belief, or preference. If an ethical theory is to have any weight at all, it must be grounded in reasons that most sensible people would be willing to accept. Of course, it helps to have other rational people with whom to discuss and debate moral issues; otherwise ethical discourse becomes extremely difficult.

What does it mean to engage in rational moral discourse? In general, there are three essential steps involved in developing a rational argument: (1) Start from reasonable principles; (2) Argue logically from those principles; (3) Strive to be factually accurate.

Start from reasonable principles. For example, we might start with a principle like, "It is morally wrong to kill an innocent human being." This principle, while certainly lofty, would probably be accepted by most reasonable people. In fact, the conviction that innocent human life must always be protected is the moral cornerstone of most religious traditions. It is only in rather extreme cases—for example, where a family decides to withdraw life support from a patient who has been comatose for many years—that we might have some debate about whether or not this principle should be accepted absolutely.

Argue logically from those principles. Starting from our basic principle, we might then argue the following:

- It is morally wrong to kill an innocent human being.
- Abortion is the killing of an innocent human being.
- Therefore abortion is morally wrong.

The argument used above is what is known as a valid argument. What this means is that the conclusion of the argument follows necessarily from the premises. If you accept the premises, you are obligated to accept the conclusion as well. Many people might also say that the argument is sound. A sound argument is one in which the conclusion follows necessarily from the premises and the premises are also true. There are perfectly rational people, however, who would dispute the truth of the claim that the fetus is actually a human being. In attacking the truth of the second premise, the basic soundness of the argument gets thrown into question. In ethical discourse it is extremely important to strive to use arguments that are both valid and sound. Failure to do so will almost inevitably mean that your moral position will not be taken seriously by other people no matter how worthy it might otherwise be.

Strive to be factually accurate. We also need to be sure that the facts, data, and statistics that we use in our moral arguments are true and accurate. Never use facts that are made up or which you know to be wrong just to score some debate points with an opponent. The following argument made by Rush Limbaugh on his radio show is a good illustration of how some individuals use false information in order to persuade others: "Liberal tree huggers," says Limbaugh, "want to prevent any kind of logging because they say that the country is becoming deforested. But there are more trees in the country today than there were 100 years ago. So what is the problem with allowing folks to do a little logging in federal lands?"

The problem with this argument is that Limbaugh is playing fast and loose with his facts. Most ecologists will tell you that it is certainly not the case that there are more trees in the United States today than there were one hundred years ago and that many of the new trees that have been planted in the country are not the "old growth" kind that can sustain wildlife. When we use erroneous facts like this to bolster our moral

theory, we do an incredible injustice to that theory and ultimately undermine our ability to persuade others.

The Example of Socrates. Look at the arguments that Socrates makes
in defending his position to remain in prison. Does he start from reasonable principles? If so, what are those principles? Does he argue logically
from those principles? Check to see if the arguments that he uses are
both valid and sound. Finally, is he attempting to be factually accurate in
the specific statements that he uses in arguments? I think that we would
have to say that Socrates meets the criteria for rational discourse rather nicely in the arguments that he presents to Crito. One could quibble
about whether all of Socrates' premises are in fact true—for example,
is the relationship of an individual to his state really like that between
a child and his parent?—but the arguments as a whole have struck people throughout the centuries as being persuasive. If they weren't, most
people would think of Socrates as a fanatic rather than a morally heroic
individual whose example is worthy of emulation.

2. Openness

If the ethical theory that you espouse is truly rational, then you should be
able to enter into moral arguments even with those who espouse views
different from your own. You should also be open to the possibility that
individuals with whom you are arguing may very well be able to persuade you of the merits of their theory and force you to abandon your
own. Remember, our basic assumption is that other people are just as
rational as you are. If we accept this assumption as true then we must
acknowledge that we may be able to learn something about the moral
life from our opponents. Even in those cases where someone else's moral
theory may come into conflict with our own, at the very least, we must
be open to the idea that his or her perspective can at least influence ours.

Unfortunately, most people enter into moral debates assuming that
their own theory is perfect and that they will be the ones to persuade others to change their moral perspectives. How many times have you had an
argument with someone only to realize that he was simply not listening
to what you were saying because his mind had already been made up
on the issue being discussed? This kind of rigid and dogmatic attitude
makes doing ethics extremely difficult, if not impossible. It also prevents
individuals from attaining moral maturity by preventing their own ethical perspective from evolving.

The Example of Socrates. In the selection from the *Crito* used above,
it would seem that Socrates really isn't all that open to the numerous

points that Crito raises about why Socrates should escape from prison (e.g., people will think that Crito is too cheap or cowardly to save Socrates; Socrates' enemies would gloat at his misfortune; his family will suffer if he dies). The problem with Crito's arguments, and the very reason why Socrates dismisses them so quickly, is that they really aren't arguments (logoi) at all, but rather groundless opinions (doxa). Crito's opinions are appeals to Socrates' emotions rather than to reason, they are not backed-up by the persuasive force of logic and rationality, and they place far too much emphasis on the empty beliefs of the majority. But, as Socrates himself puts it, he is the kind of man "who must be guided by reason, whatever the reason may be which upon reflection appears to me to be the best." Like Socrates, we are called to be open to the rational arguments of other people, but we need not spend endless amounts of time weighing the thoughtless opinions of those who prefer to make empty rhetorical pronouncements rather than use rational argumentation.

3. Universality

Most ethicists would also maintain that a viable ethical theory should also be universal in scope. Ethical theories are almost always articulated in the form of general rules of behavior. These rules are usually expressed in the form of a statement like, "Everyone ought to do x." But as Robert Solomon points out, the question of universality does raise some difficulties. Does the everyone included in this statement mean "everyone in the world, or everyone in this society, or everyone 'like us,' or, the most trivial, everyone who is in the same relevant circumstance?" (11)

A cultural relativist, for example, would have serious problems with the idea that moral principles transcend cultural barriers. They would argue that, while we can say an act is right or wrong for individuals in our society, it is extremely arrogant to presume that this moral judgment holds true for people in other societies as well.

The Example of Socrates. Socrates, however, clearly believed that moral judgments were universal in scope and should apply to all people at all times. The arguments that he develops for Crito are as applicable to those of us living today as they were to people in ancient Athens. The idea that one ought never to intentionally cause harm to another human being, which is the major premise of Socrates first argument, has been accepted as a universal principle for ethics throughout the centuries. We may debate whether or not one should accept this principle absolutely, but there is no question of its universal application.

As Socrates realized, if one's moral theory only applies to oneself or to a small group of individuals, then one's moral system becomes fairly superficial. Thus, we have to, at least, start with the assumption that moral principles are absolute and apply to everyone. Practical application will show us whether or not this is, in fact, the case.

4. Impartiality

If a moral theory is truly universal, then it must apply impartially to everyone. The principle of impartiality forbids us from treating one person differently from another when there is no legitimate reason for doing so.

This principle has been stated by Henry Sidgwick in the following way: "It cannot be right for A to treat B in a manner in which it would be wrong for B to treat A, merely on the grounds that they are different individuals, and without there being any difference between the natures and circumstances of the two that can be stated as a reasonable ground for the difference" (380). Therefore, the same moral rules that we demand others follow should apply equally to ourselves and to those close to us.

There are those, however, who believe that the requirement for impartiality in ethics is unnatural and perhaps even immoral. To illustrate the problems inherent in treating people impartially, let's examine the following, admittedly extreme, situation: imagine that on his way home a man comes upon two individuals trapped in a burning building. One is his daughter, a simple cleaning woman by profession; the other is a Nobel prize-winning scientist who is working on a cure for cancer. If this individual was trying to be completely impartial, he would have to recognize that the scientist's life was worth more objectively than that of his daughter, and he ought to save him rather than her. John Cottingham has argued that the person who acts in an impartial manner in such a circumstance is nothing more than a "moral leper" ("Partiality" 357).

He goes on to question whether the attempt to be impartial in our moral decision making is even possible. "Personal bonds, ties of affection, family ties," he argues, "are like the intimate concern one necessarily has for one's own body, an unavoidable part of what it is to be a human being. To say that the moral outlook is one which should attempt to ignore or transcend these bonds is to propose a concept of morality which seems inconsistent with our very humanity" ("Ethics" 89). For Cottingham, then, it is perfectly natural and completely moral for us to treat those close to us differently than we would less intimate others or strangers.

The Example of Socrates. Although Cottingham's position seems intuitively correct, Socrates once again provides us with an alternative perspective on this issue. As we have already seen, Socrates clearly believes that the arguments that he develops for Crito are universal in scope. Because they are universal, Socrates doesn't hesitate to apply them to himself first and foremost, and as a result could not justify escaping from prison. Nor does he allow the unenviable position of his family, who would be left to fend for themselves if he was executed, deter him from doing what he believed to be right.

We might be inclined to treat those we like with greater moral favoritism than other individuals or apply a different set of moral standards when dealing with each group, but Socrates' example shows that, if we are serious about the moral life, we will strive to treat others in much the same way that we would treat ourselves or intimate others. If it is wrong to lie, for example, then it is as wrong to lie in our business dealings as it would be to lie to our family members. This is not to say that our attempts at applying moral rules impartially will be easy or that we will always be successful. It simply means that the goal of treating all those we have dealings with impartially should guide our moral decision-making.

5. Practicality

A theory that is so rigid and extreme that it cannot be practically implemented by human beings is no good to anyone. This does not mean that our moral theories and principles can't be idealistic, challenging, and lofty; it only means that our moral idealism must always be balanced by a practical consideration: can real human beings actually live according to such principles?

For example, a theory of radical altruism that argues that one must always be concerned with the good of others with no regard for one's self is highly unrealistic (who could consistently live this way? And who would want to?). Such a theory could only frustrate the individuals attempting to live according to its principles. In the end, it would collapse under the weight of its own naive idealism.

When you are developing your own moral principles, then, it is extremely important to ask yourself one crucial question: can a person with the highest moral standards live according to this principle? If it would be difficult even for an ethical giant to follow your principles, then it is reasonable to assume that you will have difficulty living according to them.

The Example of Socrates. There are those who maintain that Socrates' own moral approach was too rigid, and that, if he had only been a bit more reasonable and realistic, he could have gone on living a comfortable life in some other Greek city-state rather than facing death though hemlock poisoning. The problem with this position is that it fails to recognize that Socrates had already spent years thinking about the reasonability of his moral way of life in light of the possibility of being killed by members of his society who were incensed by his endless interrogations. He was convinced that, if he maintained his moral integrity, he had nothing at all to fear from death. Reflecting on the possibilities surrounding death in his *Apology* (his defense speech to the Athenian jury that was trying him), he spells out the options in the following way:

> Let us reflect in another way, and we shall see that there is great reason to hope that death is a good, for one of two things:—either death is a state of nothingness and utter unconsciousness, or, as men say, there is a change and migration of the soul from this world to another. Now if you suppose that there is no consciousness, but a sleep like the sleep of him who is undisturbed even by the sight of dreams, death will be an unspeakable gain. For if a person were to select the night in which his sleep was undisturbed even by dreams, and were to compare with this the other days and nights of his life, and then were to tell us how many days and nights he had passed in the course of his life better and more pleasantly than this one, I think that any man...will not find many such days or nights, when compared with the others. Now if death is like this, I say that death is a gain; for eternity is then only a single night. But if death is a journey to another place, and there, as men say, all the dead are, what good, O my friends and judges, can be greater than this?...What would not a man give if he might converse with Orpheus and Musaeus and Hesiod and Homer? Nay, if this be true, let me die again and again.
>
> Wherefore, O judges, be of good cheer about death, and know this of a truth—that no evil can happen to a good man either in this life or after death. He and his are not neglected by the gods....
>
> The hour of departure has arrived, and we go our ways—I to die, and you to live. Which is better God only knows (Apology 40c–42a).

Socrates clearly believed that, if he maintained his moral integrity in this life, he would reap the rewards in the next. Although he is not certain what awaits him after death (an eternal slumber or an afterlife with the gods and heroes of Greece), he was convinced that whatever happened was nothing to fear and that "the good man cannot be harmed" in this life or the next.

So when we consider Socrates' ethics in light of his views on death and the afterlife, his position seems eminently pragmatic. We might disagree once again about whether his views on this matter are sound, but we cannot deny that if death is nothing to be feared than it is not quite so unreasonable to maintain one's moral convictions, even if these convictions might cause one to be executed, as Socrates eventually was.

Another Challenge

In this chapter, I have laid out what many ethicists consider the essential characteristics of a viable moral theory. In the second part of this text, you will be given the opportunity to examine some of the most influential moral theories in Western ethics. You might find some of these persuasive and others completely unconvincing. As you examine each of these theories, I would ask you to consider whether it meets the characteristics for a viable moral theory described above.

Of course, if none of the theories presented in this text meets with your approval, you are more than welcome to try to develop your own moral theory. Just be sure that it meets the criteria that we have just discussed.

For Further Discussion

1. Examine the following moral arguments and explain whether or not they are logically sound:

    *   Intentionally taking the life of a human being is morally wrong. But war by its very nature always involves the intentional taking of human life. Therefore, no war can ever be morally justified.

    *   Whatever saves a human life is justified. Experimentation on animals saves human lives. Therefore experimentation on animals is morally justifiable.

    *   Society has an obligation to prevent harm from occurring to its citizens. Citizens are harmed all the time from smoking. Therefore society has an obligation to ban smoking.

    *   People ought to be free to do whatever the hell they want as long

as they don't hurt other people. The free exchange of money for sex (prostitution) doesn't hurt anyone. Therefore prostitution should be permitted in our society.

- Individuals have a right to determine when and how to end their lives. The state's prohibition against physician assisted suicide is an infringement upon this basic right. Therefore, the state's prohibition against physician-assisted suicide is wrong.

- God's will ought to be followed at all times by human beings. The Bible represents God's will as it has been revealed to human beings. Therefore the precepts and rules laid out in the Bible ought to be followed by all human beings.

2. A Moral Debate: Miranda, Susan, Todd, Cortney and Glen are philosophy majors at Sacramento State College. One night while they are hanging out in Todd's dorm room, they enter into a debate on the ethics of the death penalty. Read the following transcript of their discussion and explain which of our rules for a viable ethical theory are broken during the course of the discussion.

- Miranda: "In order for a society to function effectively, all of its members need to know that those who commit violent crimes will be punished swiftly and severely. The death penalty sends a message to would-be offenders that if you take an innocent human life, yours will be taken as well, and therefore acts as a potent deterrent to other would-be violent offenders. After all, if you know you would be strung up, you sure as hell wouldn't stab someone you were having an argument with, would you?"

- Susan: "Well, in general I agree with you that the state has the right to take the life of those convicted of first degree murder. My cousin Lupe, though, is in prison right now for poisoning her boyfriend. She found out that he was cheating on her with her best friend and served him an arsenic cocktail just to teach him a lesson. Poor Lupe. She has had such bad luck in her relationships with guys that you just can't blame her for what she did."

- Todd: "Well, I think that we ought to live in a society in which all human beings' fundamental rights are respected, and this includes those convicted of violent crimes like murder. I simply don't believe that it pays to punish violent offenders, because all this does is prove that we as a society are unable to rehabilitate them. Instead I think that we ought to house such individuals with nurturing families so that they can receive the love that they never received from their own families."

- Glen: "What is wrong with you, Todd! The Lord has said, 'An eye for an eye, a tooth for a tooth.' God wills that those who commit violent crimes suffer by having their lives taken. You are such a damn idealist; there is no use even listening to you!"

- Cortney: "Calm down, Glen. There is a compromise position available. The Catholic Church, for example, has argued that, while the death penalty is morally wrong, it can be used in those societies where there is not the means available to incarcerate those convicted of murder. So, while use of the death penalty wouldn't be acceptable in the U.S. or in Europe, it could be used in many other countries throughout the world."

3. Imagine that you were involved in the discussion. Do you think you could develop an argument for or against the death penalty that would satisfy all of the requirements described in this chapter for a viable ethical theory?

Sources and Further Reading

Cohen, Stephen. *The Nature of Moral Reasoning*. New York: Oxford University Press, 2004.

Cottingham, John. "Ethics and Impartiality." *Philosophical Studies* 43 (1983): 83-99

—. "Partiality, Favourtism, and Morality." *Philosophical Quarterly* 36 (1986): 357-373.

Plato. *The Republic and Other Works*. Trans. Benjamin Jowett. New York: Doubleday, 1989.

Sidgwick, Henry. The Methods of Ethics. Indianapolis, IN: Hackett, 1981.

Solomon, Robert. *On Ethics and Living Well*. Belmont, CA: Wadsworth, 2006.

Taylor, Paul. "On Taking the Moral Point of View." *Midwest Studies in Philosophy* 3 (1978): 35-61.

Wallace, Gerald and Walker, A.D.M., eds. *The Definition of Morality*. London: Metheun, 1970.

Williams, Bernard. *Ethics and the Limits of Philosophy*. Cambridge: Harvard University Press, 1985.

PART TWO

THE GREAT ETHICAL THEORIES

INTRODUCING THE GREAT ETHICAL THEORIES

Case Study: To Squeal or Not to Squeal

Rosario Dominguez is a mid-level manager in the Customer Services Division of Kidco, a nationally recognized company that manufactures high-end children's toys out of wood. Recently, however, the new CEO of Kidco has decided that in order to compete with chains such as Fischer-Price and Mattel, the company needs to cut its manufacturing costs dramatically. To accomplish this goal Kidco is now sending its toys to be painted in China instead of at its own U.S. plants, where labor costs are much higher.

About eight months after these new toys started appearing on toy store shelves, an article appeared in the New York Times stating that three employees at the company handed over documents showing that several popular Kidco toys were painted in China using lead-based paints, which are outlawed in the U.S. because of the health risks associated with lead. The company is facing potential fines and lawsuits that could cause it to lose millions of dollars and perhaps even force it to reduce much of its workforce in the U.S. In order to mount a successful public relations campaign, the company needs to find out who the whistle-blowers are and to discredit them publicly by showing that their actions are politically motivated.

Investigators for the company have reason to suspect three disgruntled employees in Customer Services and they approach Rosario, asking if she has any knowledge about whether these three leaked the story to the Times. In fact, one of these suspected workers, Lori Grunthal, had confided to Rosario that she and the two others are indeed the whistle-blowers that the company is looking for, but made Rosario promise not to tell anyone. Rosario knows that if she rats out her colleagues, she will probably be promoted by the company as a reward, but that her three co-workers will certainly pay a severe price for speaking out against the company. Although the management of Kidco could not directly re-taliate against these employees because of federal whistle-blower laws, Rosairo knows that they would use any opportunity the could to make life miserable for these workers and ultimate drive them from the company.

For Discussion

Answer the following questions as succinctly as possible:

1. In this specific case the right thing for Rosario to do would be...

2. The reason why this is the right thing to do is because...

What Makes an Act Right or Wrong?

Obviously the case presented above is a difficult one because there are so many conflicting values and interests at stake. Different people will likely view the moral dimension of this case in radically different ways and perhaps come up with conflicting interpretations of how Rosario should behave.

How did you answer the questions posed above? You were asked to specify what you believed would be the right thing for Rosario to do in this case, and then to justify your position. To put this in more theoretical terms, you were asked to explain what makes a human act morally right or wrong. Clearly, this is no simple question and has been the source of considerable debate throughout the history of philosophy. In answering the question of what precisely makes an act right or wrong, you are, in fact, doing nothing less than establishing the basic moral principle that you believe should guide all moral action. You are engaged, in other words, in the great project of moral philosophers throughout the centuries.

Now that I've frightened you a bit with the complexity of this undertaking, it is your turn to establish the basic moral principle that you believe should guide all human action. As you consider your answer to this question, you may want to think through various moral acts that you have performed in your own life and what it was that made them right or wrong:

```
┌─────────────────────────────────────────────────────┐
│                                                       │
│              An act is morally right if...            │
│                                                       │
│                                                       │
│                                                       │
│                                                       │
│                                                       │
│                                                       │
│                                                       │
└─────────────────────────────────────────────────────┘
```

Searching for Objective Criteria

We have seen that one of the problems with a moral system like subjectivism is that it provides no objective basis for determining which actions are right or wrong in different circumstances. If certain acts are right and others are wrong, then there must be some kind of objective basis for making such a determination.

Take the example of drug use, for instance. As we have seen, it is not enough simply to say that drug use is wrong simply because one may find the practice personally repugnant or that it is morally acceptable simply because one approves of the act. There has to be some kind of objective criteria that we can point to about the act that makes it right or wrong.

For illustrative purposes, let's take a look at two very different approaches to ethics:

A religious conservative might argue that drug use is morally wrong because God has condemned the use of such intoxicants. So the basic objective principle that he is operating under would be something like this:

"An act is morally right if, and only if, the act is consistent with what God commands."

While there are problems with this principle that were raised in Chapter 3, at least the advocate of religious conservatism can point to some more or less objective basis for maintaining that drug use is wrong. There might be some debate among believers about what God actually commands (the evidence from scripture is often ambiguous or inconclusive when it comes to many moral issues), but at least those who espouse this theory have a clear starting point for moral discussion.

Let's say we have a different objective basis for moral decision making. Perhaps we are ethical hedonists for whom the greatest good is to attain as much pleasure in life as possible. Naturally, there are some serious issues with this sort of approach to ethics as well, but, for now, let's just accept the possible validity of this approach. The hedonist may very well argue that drug use is morally acceptable because he is operating from the following principle:

> *"An act is morally right if, and only if, the act produces the greatest amount of pleasure for oneself."*

If you are a hedonist, then, any act which produces pleasure for yourself and avoids inflicting pain would be considered morally good. Of course, later on the hedonist may have to make some distinctions between immediate- and long-term pleasure, and decide which of these is the most important, but that is unimportant right now.

You are probably getting the point by now. When examining any ethical theory, it is important first to understand the basic objective criteria that the theory uses to determine in every imaginable circumstance which actions are right and which actions are wrong.

The Big Theories

For the remainder of this text we are going to be focusing on the five ethical theories that have had the greatest impact in Western moral thought: ethical egoism, utilitarianism, deontology, rights theory, and virtue ethics. Although there are many other theories we could also examine, these five are considered the "biggies" in the field of ethics. It is probably also the case that most people's own moral perspectives have been shaped and influenced by at least one of these main theories.

In a nutshell, here are the objective criteria that each of these theories fall back on:

> ***Ethical Egoism:*** "An act is morally right if, more than any other alternative available at the time, it brings about the greatest amount of good, or happiness, for oneself."

> ***Utilitarianism***: "An act is morally right if, more than any other alternative available at the time, it brings about the greatest amount of good, or happiness, for all those who are affected by the act."

Deontology: "An act is morally right if it accords with a universal rule that all can follow."

Rights Theory: "An act is morally right if, in performing it, one does not violate the basic rights of others."

Virtue Ethics: "An act is morally right if it is performed by a person of virtuous moral character."

In general, we can fit all of these theories into two main categories: consequentialist theories and non-consequentialist theories. Consequentialist theories, such as ethical egoism and utilitarianism look to the consequences of an act to determine if that act is right or wrong. Non-consequentialist theories, such as deontology, rights theory and virtue ethics, maintain that the rightness or wrongness of an act have nothing to do with the consequences of the act, but rather have to do with something intrinsic to the act itself.

So now that you have an overview of the BIG ETHICAL THEORIES, we can examine each of them in detail. Although each of these theories has its benefits as well as its limitations, in the end you are the one who will have to determine which system makes the most sense for you.

For Further Discussion

1. The Bergmeier Case: The "Bergmeier Case," developed by John Keenan, is a notable one in contemporary Moral Theology. As you read the case, explain what you think would be the morally correct course of action for Mrs. Bergmeier. But more importantly, be prepared to justify your answer based upon some kind of moral principle you think people ought to follow:

    > Mrs. Bergmeier is a married woman with several children and a husband who is ill. She has been arrested by the Nazis for assisting her Jewish neighbors and sentenced to six years without parole. After months in the camp, she learns that her husband's health is progressively declining due to his tending to the children, and that the children are not faring at all well due to their father's ailing state.
    >   She also learns something else: because of overcrowding, the

camp releases pregnant women who are held for lesser crimes, like hers. Aware of one particular guard who regularly makes outrageous advances on her, Mrs. Bergmeier, for the sake of her family, submits herself to him. Three months later a pregnant Mrs. Bergmeier returns to her family to care for her husband and children.

2. Case Studies: Consider the following situations and explain whether or not you believe that the actions described are morally right or wrong in light of the basic moral principle that you selected earlier in this chapter.

    •   Marg Scherer and Walt Kaslow are competing for a managerial position at Kreskey's Department Store. Both are equally qualified and have been at the company the same number of years. Mr. Dellapisio, the store's general manger, decides that Kaslow should get the job because, based upon his experiences, he believes men in general are more dedicated to their jobs than women.

    •   Milton Barowski owns a failing cellophane production plant in Missouri. Because of poor business decisions that he has made, Milton has more debt than he can possibly repay. He realizes, however, that the fire insurance on his plant will be enough to repay all of his debts. One evening, when he is sure that no one is in the plant, he lights a fire in the plant, burning it to the ground.

    •   The State Environmental Protection Agency of Arkansas has mandated that hog farms treat pig waste in an environmentally sustainable manner. The approved methods of handling this waste typically cost hog farmers millions of dollars a year--costs which are normally passed on to the consumer. John Alfano owns a pig farm in Arkansas that employs 150 low-skilled workers. Because of rising costs, he is concerned that he will not be able to remain competitive if he follows the EPA's guidelines. Taking advantage of a loop-hole in the law, he allows the pig waste to seep into a nearby river. Although he believes that the quantities of pig waste he is allowing to enter the river will not be harmful to humans, he knows that it will have a negative impact on fish populations in the river.

    •   Marie Swaine is a physician in Delaware, where the use of marijuana, even for medical purposes, is illegal. Studies that she has read convince her that smoking marijuana can ease the severity of certain ill effects of cancer. She believes that several of her patients would profit from this treatment. She decides to make marijuana available to them, even though it is clearly against the law and could put her medical license in jeopardy.

Sources and Further Reading

Frankena, William. *Ethics.* Englewood Cliffs, NJ: Prentice Hall, 2001.
Keenan, James F. "Proposing Cardinal Virtues." *Theological Studies* 56 (1995).
Pojman, Louis. *Ethics: Discovering Right and Wrong.* Belmont, CA: Wadsworth, 2002.
Rachels, James. *The Elements of Moral Philosophy.* New York: McGraw-Hill, 2002.
Timmons, Mark. *Moral Theory.* Lanham, MD: Rowman and Littlefield, 2002.
Williams, Bernard. *Morality: An Introduction to Ethics.* New York: Harper & Row, 1972.

ETHICAL EGOISM

Case Study: A Matter of Choice

Denise Samos is a biology major at Monroe College in Rockland County, New York. For some time now she has had a crush on Matt Reich, a pre-med student at her college. Denise is not only physically attracted to Matt, but during conversations with him she has found him to be warm, funny, and very smart. In short, Matt is exactly the kind of guy that Denise would love to be dating if she had the choice. Unfortunately, just about every other girl at the college also finds Matt to be incredibly desirable, so Denise has been forced to resign herself to the fact that she and Matt will probably have to remain just friends.

One day during one of their bio labs, Matt casually mentions to Denise that he has managed to score two tickets to a Bob Dylan concert for the following evening, Thursday night, at Madison Square Garden—a real coup considering how hard these tickets are to come by. Matt knows from previous conversations that Denise, like himself, is a fanatical Dylan fan, and thought it might be fun if they went together. Needless to say, Denise was ecstatic about the offer, not just because she loves Dylan, but also because she thinks that this event might possibly lead to a more intimate relationship with Matt than she currently has.

There is one hitch, however. Denise has a very good friend named Marta, whom she has known since childhood and who also is a biology major at Monroe. Marta has been having a considerable amount of trouble with an Advanced Genetics course that she has been taking and is afraid that if she fails the midterm that is scheduled for this Friday, she will flunk out of the program. Marta's parents are hard-working immigrants from Colombia, who have little formal education of their own but who have managed to run a fairly profitable meat processing plant in upstate New York. They clearly don't think much of Marta's dreams of becoming a biology teacher and have told her that they will allow her to remain in college as long as she does well. Marta knows that if she fails out of the biology program her parents will use this as an excuse to insist that she leave college and come work in the family business—which she hates—as an assistant to her father.

Because Denise had already taken Advanced Biology and did very well in it, she had previously offered to spend Thursday afternoon and evening coaching Marta for the exam. Denise knows that with her knowledge of the subject matter, she can help Marta pass the exam and make it through the biology program.

Denise has to make a choice: help her dear friend study for this crucial exam or go with Matt to the Dylan concert and, perhaps, begin a relationship with him. Naturally she is torn by this decision and comes to you for your advice.

For Discussion

What decision would you advise Denise to make? If Denise chooses to help her friend, Marta, do you think that this is evidence that she is behaving in a purely selfless way? Why or why not? If Denise decides to go with Matt to the concert, would there be anything morally wrong with this decision? If so, what?

In attempting to discern principles that can guide us in our ethical decision-making, we have already seen that we have numerous options from which to choose. The most intuitive place to start, I think, is with an approach to ethics that appeals to our basic human instinct to promote our own self-interest above and beyond all other concerns. The general term used for such theories is "egoism," but egoistic theories can come in either of two main forms—psychological egoism or ethical egoism. The differences between these two theories can be summed up in the following way:

- Psychological Egoism is a descriptive theory which states that human beings cannot help but behave selfishly, and, therefore, altruism is an illusion.

- Ethical Egoism is a normative theory which states that human beings ought to behave selfishly, and, therefore, altruism is foolish.

The main distinction, then, between these two theories lies in the fact that psychological egoism is a purely descriptive theory that describes how human beings presumably behave; ethical egoism, on the other hand, is a normative theory that prescribes how human beings ought to behave. One theory says that human beings are selfish; the other that human beings ought to be selfish. Psychological egoism is not a moral theory per se, but it does have interesting applications to ethics, which are definitely worth considering before we turn to our discussion of ethical egoism.

The Theory of Psychological Egoism

The basic premise of psychological egoism has a long history in Western ethics and has influenced a great many contemporary thinkers. What is this premise? It is that human beings always behave selfishly in everything that they do, and that it is impossible for them to behave otherwise. According to this theory, even when human beings appear to be acting out of altruistic—that is, selfless—motives, they are actually acting because of some advantage or benefit that they perceive for themselves. If you were to examine the supposedly altruistic acts of individuals carefully enough, according to the psychological egoist, you will inevitably uncover a selfish motive.

To illustrate the theory of psychological egoism more clearly, let's examine two actions that on the surface appear to be inspired by quite different motives. It is Thanksgiving Day and on the south side of Chicago there are two soup kitchens that will be serving dinner to the homeless. In one soup kitchen a politician who is running for high office has donned an apron and is carving turkey in front of cameras from two local television stations. In another soup kitchen a Sister of Mercy performs the same action out of her love for God's hungry children and with virtually no recognition. Most of us would probably argue that the politician is serving food to the homeless because of some advantage that he perceives for himself—most notably, a good photo-op that will help win greater support for his campaign. But what about the Sister of Mercy? We might be tempted to say that she is acting out of purely altruistic motives and that therefore her actions are much more laudable than the politicians'. But are they really? A psychological egoist would argue that in fact there is absolutely no difference between the actions of these two individuals: both are acting out of purely selfish motives. We know that the politician is engaged in a crass effort to convince his constituency that he is compassionate so that he will be reelected, but what are the selfish motives of the Sister of Mercy? The psychological egoist might argue that she derives pleasure from the act, and that this is her motivation for acting, not concern for those in need. Or he might suggest that there is some hidden motivation that inspires her: a desire to feel that she is noble or heroic, or perhaps to earn her reward in the next life. In any case, the psychological egoist would reject the idea that she is acting altruistically, since she obviously is deriving certain benefits from the act.

Psychological Egoism is actually quite an ancient theory. An early form of it was described by Plato in his dialogue, *The Republic,* where Plato has Glaucon, one of the participants in the dialogue, formulate a very persuasive argument in support of psychological egoism. In the second book of this work, Glaucon tells the story about Gyges, a shepherd, who came upon a magic ring in a fissure caused by an earthquake. Gyges quickly discovers that the ring he has found makes its wearer invisible, enabling him to go anywhere undetected. And what does Gyges do with this ring? Help the poor and suffering? Punish the wicked? Of course not! Putting the ring on his finger, he sneaks into the royal palace, violates the Queen, murders the king and seizes the throne for himself.

Glaucon goes on to ask us to imagine what would happen if there were two such rings—one given to a person of virtue and the other to a scoundrel. Would there be any difference in the way the two would behave? We would certainly expect the scoundrel to act horrendously in the absence of any social restraint. But would the virtuous man behave any better? Glaucon argues that, freed from the threat of punishment, the virtuous man would almost certainly behave just as badly as the scoundrel. At first he might be discrete in his use of the ring and try only to use it for good purposes, but after a while he would commit acts of injustice aimed at promoting his own selfish interest. Glaucon's argument in The Republic is that all human beings are naturally selfish and unjust. When we know that we can get away with something that is to our own advantage, we will do it, no matter how harmful it might be to others. The only reason, in fact, why most people behave decently is because of the threat of punishment. If we could somehow eliminate that threat there would be no limits to our selfishness.

Contemporary theories of psychological egoism are basically a new spin on this ancient idea. Examining human action, the advocates of this theory note that even apparently unselfish acts give the one performing them a sense of satisfaction, and that self-satisfaction produces a feeling of pleasure. They then go on to argue that the real object in performing "altruistic" actions is to have this feeling of pleasure, rather than to help others. This selfish motivation is as true for the student who gives up a night on the town to help her friend study for a calculus exam as it would be for Maximilian Kolbe, who sacrificed his life in a concentration camp for the sake of someone he barely knew. Neither can be said to be acting out of real concern for other human beings.

While psychological egoism is seductive in that it offers a simple and seemingly persuasive account of human action, it has been rejected on a number of different counts.

A major objection that can be raised against psychological egoism lies in the distinction between the causes and the effects of our actions. The psychological egoist, as we have seen, rejects the possibility of altruism because he looks at an apparently altruistic act and observes that one has received benefits from performing the act (i.e., feeling of pleasure). But just because someone receives benefits from an act doesn't mean that they necessarily performed the act for the sake of those benefits. The benefits, in other words, may very well be an effect rather than a cause of the good acts. Thus a woman who stays up all night caring for her sick child, depriving herself of comfort and sleep, naturally feels pleasure at the thought that she is acting the way a good mother should. While the psychological egoist would say that the feelings of pleasure that she receives from caring for her child are the cause of her actions, doesn't it make just as much sense to say that they are rather bi-products—or effects—of her selfless act? According to this view the goal of an altruistic person is not to attain pleasure, but simply to help someone in need. When we succeed in our goal, the result is pleasure. And there is absolutely nothing at all selfish about that.

Another problem with psychological egoism is that the theory fails to recognize the complexity of human motivations. If one takes the time to look carefully at the gamut of human activity, it is apparent that human beings actually act from a wide range of different, and sometimes even conflicting, motivations. Most acts are rarely so simple that they are performed out of one sole motivation. Take the example of the teenage boy who goes out of his way to help an elderly woman cross a busy street. He may be acting out of a "selfish" motivation to feel good about himself or have others think of him in a heroic light. But he may also be acting out of guilt, because the old lady reminds him of his dead grandmother; or he may simply be acting out of compassion for someone in need. It may very well be the case, however, that all three motivations are inspiring him at the same time.

It's also the case that a person can perform the exact same act at different times for quite different reasons. On my way to work on Monday, for example, I might pass a homeless woman asking for a handout, and give her $5.00 because I feel compassion for her. Then on the way home from work on Friday, I might see the same woman, and again give her $5.00. This time, though, my act is motivated purely out of a selfish desire not to be confronted by her humanity before the relaxing weekend that I have planned for myself. Finally, we have seen that the exact same act—serving Thanksgiving dinner—can be performed by two different people with very different motivations: the politician seeking self-promotion and the Sister of Mercy seeking to minister to individuals in need. The problem with psychological egoism is that it represents a shallow approach to understanding the complexity of human motivations. In reducing all motivation to selfishness, the psychological egoist turns all human actions to something banal and trite. And human actions, as we are all well aware, are anything but banal and trite.

All of these quite valid objections must inevitably make us conclude that, in its absolute form, psychological egoism is a fairly flawed theory of human motivation. Still, the theory does force us to reflect on what actually drives us to perform certain actions which might on the surface appear selfless. We certainly like to think that when we do something kind or generous for someone else we are acting out of purely altruistic motivations. But is this necessarily true? The psychological egoist would ask us to examine our deeper motivations to see what the real source of our actions is. While the psychological egoist may go a bit too far in rejecting even the possibility of a truly selfless act, certainly, as we have seen, our motivations for helping others is quite often mixed at best. It's also the case that quite often we deceive ourselves into thinking that we are doing something selfless, when in fact our true motivations might actually be much less noble than we'd care to believe. This is not to say that we can never be purely altruistic; just that we are probably motivated less by altruistic inclinations than we may think we are.

The Theory of Ethical Egoism

While psychological egoism can be discounted as a viable ethical theory, there is another type of egoistic theory that is much more useful in providing us with guidance in our human behavior. This is the normative theory of ethical egoism. Although there are not too many people who call themselves ethical egoists, the theory serves as the ethical underpinning for a political and economic theory that is highly influential in the United States—libertarianism. We'll return to discuss libertarianism in the third part of this text, but it should be kept in mind that much of our public policy in the United States has been shaped by that libertarian conviction that individuals should be allowed to maximize their own self-interest, a conviction which is essentially founded upon the principles of ethical egoism.

The basic principle that an ethical egoist would follow when determining how he should act would be something like this:

> Everyone ought to act so as to bring about the greatest amount of good, or happiness, for him or herself.

Every other theory that we examine in this text will maintain that the well-being of others is just as important as our own well-being (the radical altruist goes even further, arguing that the well-being of others is even more important than our own). Ethical egoism, on the other hand, argues that the well-being of others is an irrelevant consideration when we are determining how we ought to behave. Instead, we ought to pursue our own good with no thought to how it might benefit or harm others.

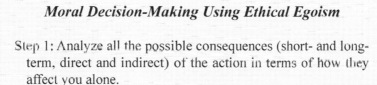

Moral Decision-Making Using Ethical Egoism

Step 1: Analyze all the possible consequences (short- and long-term, direct and indirect) of the action in terms of how they affect you alone.

Step 2: Determine if the action, more than any other alternative available at the time, will produce the greatest amount of good, or happiness, for you.

Step 3: If it does, then the act is morally right; if it doesn't, then the act is morally wrong.

Ethical egoism is above all a rational system for the promotion of one's own interests. This means that an intelligent ethical egoist would certainly not try to satisfy immediate desires at the expense of his long-term interests. For example, although it certainly might be pleasant to hang out at the beach instead of attending a boring ethics class, a true ethical egoist would know that his greater good is to be served by suffering through the class so that he can get a more fulfilling career later on in life.

This same rational approach to promoting one's own self-interest also means that an ethical egoist would probably not treat people indecently or unjustly. If he did treat people so callously, it might backfire on him, since the egoist's victims would either avoid him like the plague or work to undermine him. A sensible egoist, therefore, would probably want to treat at least some people well, but he would always do so only with the thought of what he can get back from them at a later date. In certain cases, in fact, he might even choose to sacrifice his own well-being when the long-term advantages of doing so outweighs the sacrifices he is forced to make.

Finally, although an ethical egoist wouldn't accept the idea that we have any moral obligations to our fellow human beings, he would not necessarily have any problem with individuals freely choosing to help the disadvantaged. He merely would argue that this should be done in the form of private charity, rather than through government programs involving the transfer of wealth in which the individual has no choice at all. If one were to raise the issue of what we should do to help starving children in Africa, for example, an ethical egoist would probably respond, "If you want to go help starving children in Africa, then go do it. Nothing is stopping you."

Several different sorts of arguments have been advanced by ethical egoists to support the truth of their theory:

The Natural Argument. In advancing his theory, the ethical egoist might point to nature to demonstrate that in the natural world various species selfishly pursue their goals with no thought to the well-being of other species or even members of their own species. In the end, the strong thrive and the weak perish, and the entire natural system benefits. What works for animals, argues the ethical egoist, would work equally well for human beings if we could just put aside our concern for the well-being of others and follow our natural (i.e., selfish) tendencies.

The Argument from Human Happiness. An interesting argument in favor of ethical egoism has been developed by Harry Browne that challenges the connection made by most of the world's religions between altruism and human happiness. We have seen that those who advocate an ideal of altruism argue that the world would be a better place if everyone were unselfish. Browne, however, uses an example to illustrate what the consequences would be if everyone sacrificed their own happiness for the sake of the happiness of others:

> Let's imagine that happiness is symbolized by a big red rubber ball. I have the ball in my hands, meaning that I hold the ability to be happy. But since I'm not going to be selfish, I quickly pass the ball to you. I have given up my happiness for you. What will you

do? Since you're not selfish either, you won't keep the ball; you'll quickly pass it on to your next-door neighbor. But he doesn't want to be selfish either, so he passes it on to his wife, who likewise gives it to her children. The children have been taught the virtue of unselfishness, so they pass it to playmates, who pass it to parents, who pass it to neighbors, and on and on and on.

To use a more realistic example, we might speculate what the world would be like if everyone acted like Mother Teresa, sacrificing their own happiness for others. According to Browne's argument, no one would be left to be the recipient of our generosity, and our attempts at altruism would be an exercise in futility. If we really are concerned about our own happiness, then we would be much better off hanging on to the big red ball (i.e., focusing on what makes us happy) than passing it on to others.

A related argument that Browne and other ethical egoists use is based upon the overall benefit of having each individual pursue his or her own self-interest. The argument goes like this: I know full well what makes me happy, but I really can't know what makes other people happy. If I spend my time trying to make others happy, therefore, I will probably fail in my attempt. But if I work on satisfying my own happiness, then I stand a very good chance of success.

The Economic Argument. The economic version of ethical egoism, which is known as libertarianism, supports a form of laissez-faire capitalism—that is, completely unregulated capitalism in which individuals are free to maximize their own wealth with limited government interference. The idea here is that if individuals are left alone to pursue their own economic self-interest everyone will benefit. This idea gained popularity during the Regan years under the name of "trickle-down economics." There are still a great many economists and political thinkers, however, who continue to argue that allowing individuals to focus on their own economic self-interests with limited government interference is the ideal way to maximize prosperity and happiness.

Political Ethical Egoism: Libertarianism

The political version of ethical egoism typically goes by the name of libertarianism. Although this political philosophy can take on many different, and often contradictory, forms—from radical anarchism to right-wing conservatism—all libertarians take as their starting point the basic premise of ethical egoism—namely, that the primary obligation that human beings have is to promote their own "rational self-interest" and happiness. Placing a strong emphasis on individual freedom and the right of self-determination, libertarians also argue that human beings have the absolute right to decide for themselves how they are going to live their lives without any undue interference from others.

Libertarians typically recognize three—and usually only three—basic rights: the rights to life, liberty and property. These rights are viewed as being absolute, and demand forbearance (restraint) on the part of others not to violate them:

The Right to Life. Each person has the right to dispose of his life as he sees fit. Anyone—and this includes the government—who attempts to take a person's life or injure him in any way through physical violence is violating that person's basic right to life. On the other hand, most libertarians would recognize the right of individuals to end their own lives if they see fit and therefore oppose laws prohibiting suicide and voluntary euthanasia.

The Right to Liberty. Libertarians place a great emphasis on individual liberty, which they view as the cornerstone of any civilized society. A person, they argue, has the right to live as he sees fit, as long as he doesn't interfere with anyone else's right to do the same. Libertarians object to any limitations placed upon freedom of speech, freedom of the press, freedom of assembly, and the right to own, manufacture, or sell weapons (including concealed weapons or assault weapons). They also believe that there should be no censorship of the media by the government. Although libertarians support the idea that every woman has the right to decide whether or not to have an abortion, they do not believe that taxpayers should be forced to pay for such procedures.

The Right to Property. Libertarians also emphasize the almost absolute right of individuals to use their property as they see fit, and object to any encroachments upon this right by individuals or governments (e.g., eminent domain laws, zoning ordinances, rent control, property taxes). Public lands such as national preserves and parks should be sold off for private ownership, since the government, they argue, has no business owning land.

In general, libertarians view government as a problem rather than as a solution (or, as John Hospers put it, "the most dangerous institution known to man"). Most governments, they argue, have an unfortunate history of violating human freedoms and enslaving their citizens. Therefore, the best government is the one that is most limited in scope and power. The sole role of government in libertarian political philosophy is to protect its citizens against violations of their basic rights to life, liberty, and property. Many libertarians, therefore, support taxation to provide for police protection and military defense. All other functions of government, they believe, should be privatized.

As we shall see later on in this text, libertarians reject the notion that government has any role to play in providing assistance to those who are poor or disadvantaged. As Hospers puts it:

> No one should be forced by law to help others, not even to tell them the time of day if requested, and certainly not to give them a portion of one's weekly paycheck. Governments, in the guise of humanitarianism, have given to some by taking from others ... And in doing so they have decreased incentive, violated the rights of individuals, and lowered the standards of living of almost everyone.
>
> All such laws constitute what libertarians call moral cannibalism. A cannibal in the physical sense is a person who lives off the flesh of other human beings. A *moral* cannibal is one who believes he has a right to live off the "spirit" of other human beings—who believes that he has a moral claim on the productive capacity, time, and effort expended by others (18).

Libertarians like Hospers believe that to tax the income of industrious citizens in order to help others less industrious than themselves is both immoral and unproductive. It is immoral because it confiscates the property (i.e., money) of one group of people and transfers their property to others who have no legitimate claim upon it. It is unproductive because it encourages the poor to become dependent and discourages others from working industriously to increase their own wealth.

Finally, libertarians also believe that government should not enact laws designed to prevent individuals from causing harm to themselves, rejecting the concept of "victimless crimes." Naturally, then, they oppose legal prohibitions on recreational drug use, prostitution, gambling, pornography or any kinds of sexual activities between consenting adults. They argue that government has no right to interfere in activity that harms no one else (see Libertarian National Committee).

Advantages of Ethical Egoism

Besides the philosophical arguments listed above—which are by no means inconsiderable—there are a few definite benefits that ethical egoism as a theory that make it extremely appealing to many people:

Self-interest is highly objective. Although it is extremely difficult for me to know what is in the best interest of others, I almost always know what is in my own self-interest. I am also in a much better position to determine how to satisfy my own self-interest than I would be trying to determine how to satisfy the interests of others. Ethical egoism, therefore, provides a highly objective criteria for moral action and makes it fairly easy to determine how one ought to behave in different circumstances. This is no small matter when we are confronted by serious moral dilemmas that require fairly quick moral deliberations.

Ethical egoism encourages personal responsibility. Many individuals in our society refuse to take responsibility for their own actions and look to government and their fellow citizens to lend them a helping hand when they fall on hard times. This is true even when such individuals are responsible for their own misfortunes because of bad choices that they have freely made. Ethical egoism, on the other hand, places full responsibility on the individual for maximizing their own happiness and well-being and recognizes the rights of others to do the same. Everyone, according to this theory, is completely responsible for their own success or failure in life.

Disadvantages of Ethical Egoism

Ethical egoism certainly is quite a seductive theory for many Americans. Our very way of life with its emphasis on "looking out for number one" seems to offer a practical justification for ethical egoism, as does our free-market economic system, which appears to be nothing more than ethical egoism on a national scale. But just as in the case of psychological egoism, the theory has some difficulties:

Ethical egoism is a self-defeating theory. The ethical egoist, as we have seen, advocates a theory which argues that everyone ought to promote his or her own interests regardless of the effect it has on others. It makes little sense, however, for the ethical egoist to advocate such a theory since the interests of others, if promoted, will eventually come into conflict with his own interests. Instead, a smart ethical egoist should

advise others to be scrupulously virtuous, so that he will be able to promote his own interests without competition. To be consistent, he should
actually be a champion of the purest form of altruism, rather than of
ethical egoism.

Happiness is not a zero-sum game. Ethical egoists like Brown seem
to think that there is just a limited amount of happiness to go around, and
if one focuses on the needs of others, one will necessarily be depriving
oneself. This argument ignores the fact that one's own happiness and the
happiness of others are not necessarily incompatible. In fact, there are
times when one's happiness is increased by focusing on the happiness of
others (i.e., by passing on the big red ball).

Ethical egoism is too simplistic. Another objection to ethical egoism has been raised by James Rachels who argues that both the ethical
egoist and the radical altruist offer overly simplistic views of the moral
life. Rachels adopts what he calls the common sense view, namely that
one's own interests and the interests of others are both important and
must be balanced against one another. On certain occasions, according
to Rachels, it will appear that the best thing to do is to sacrifice my own
well-being for the sake of another; on other occasions it will be perfectly
acceptable for me to work to promote my own interest. There are times,
for example, when even the best mother has a right to ask her children
to leave her alone for a half hour so that she can enjoy a book that she is
reading, while at other times she may have to make extreme sacrifices to
promote their well-being. As Rachels correctly points out, the moral life
involves finding the right balance between the two extremes of ethical
egoism and radical altruism (Rachels 88).

*Our interests can also be served by promoting the well-being of oth-
ers.* Peter Singer, a contemporary utilitarian ethicist, offers a practical
argument against ethical egoism based upon the paradoxical idea that
sometimes it is more advantageous to be altruistic than selfish. In his
work, The Expanding Circle, he begins his argument with an interesting
example:

Suppose two early humans are attacked by a sabertooth cat. If
both flee, one will be picked off by the cat; if both stand their
ground, there is a good chance that they can fight the cat off; if one
flees and the other stands and fights, the fugitive will escape and
the fighter will be killed (47-49).

Thus, if the two men in the example behaved altruistically, both would benefit in the end, but if either of them behaved selfishly, the end result would be tragedy for one of them (47-49). The implication of Singer's example is that a group of rational individuals who were out to promote their own interest will probably be better off in the long-run if they were more altruistic and less selfish.

Evaluating the Theory

As you can see, there are some quite valid reasons why you might choose to follow a moral theory like ethical egoism and some equally valid reason why this theory might be rejected. We'll encounter the same tension in all the theories that we examine in this text. Unfortunately, there's no such thing as a flawless ethical theory. Each theory we will examine has its own unique strengths and weakness, its own advantages and limitations. The question that you need to ask yourselves is whether the theory that you are examining can provide the kind of sound guidance that will enable you to live out your life in an ethical way.

In the case of ethical egoism, the strict focus on maximizing one's own self-interest with little thought to the needs and interests of others is at the same time an advantage and a disadvantage of the theory. As we've seen, ethical egoism will certainly be one of the easiest moral theories to follow, because of its great simplicity. As long as you know what is going to make you happy—and assuming that you are not deluding yourself about this—then you also know how you ought to behave.

But if you think that an ethical system must necessarily take into consideration the needs and desires of others, then you will naturally find ethical egoism a deficient moral theory. And if you believe that the needs and desires of others are at least as important as your own when attempting to decide how you ought to behave, then you'll definitely want to look for another moral theory to follow.

For Further Discussion

1. Which of the following would a supporter of ethical egoism maintain is acting morally? Be prepared to justify your answers.

   - A 37-year-old man, who is attractive enough that he is able to have sexual relations with his choice of women. After he gets tired of a woman, he simply discards her and finds another woman to take her place as his sexual partner.

- A 70-year-old multi-millionaire who has decided that, instead of leaving the bulk of his inheritance to his children, he will use the money to help find a cure for AIDS because he finds this a more meaningful use of his funds.

- A 27-year-old, who is currently unemployed and in treatment for substance abuse. This man grew up in dire poverty, in an extremely dysfunctional household, and in one of the most violent and crime-ridden communities in the country. He has been on public assistance for the past four years in order to get his life back on track.

- A 21-year-old college student who has decided that he would rather spend his time at the beach than going to classes. He will probably fail out of college this semester, but doesn't really care.

- A 24-year-old woman who has given up her own life to care for her infirmed mother, because that is what she thinks is expected of her.

2. Ethical egoists argue that society as a whole would benefit if individuals consistently pursued their own self-interest exclusively with no thought about the interests of others.

- Give some arguments to support this position.
- Give some arguments in opposition to this position.
- Do you think that the libertarian position on this issue is basically correct or not?

Sources and Further Reading

Bishop, Lloyd. *In Defense of Altruism: Inadequacies of Ayn Rand's Ethics and Psychological Egoism.* New Orleans: University Press of the South, 2001.

Broad, C.D., "Egoism as a Theory of Human Motives." *Ethics and the History of Philosophy.* New York: Humanities Press, 1952.

Brown, Harry. *How I Found Freedom in an Unfree World.* Liam Works, 1973.

Campbell, Richard. "A Short Refutation of Ethical Egoism." *Canadian Journal of Philosophy* 2 (1972): 249-254.

Feinberg, Joel. "Psychological Egoism." *Reason and Responsibility*. Ed. Joel Feinberg. Belmont, CA: Wadsworth, 1981.

Gautier, David, ed. *Morality and Rational Self-Interest*. Englewood Cliffs, NJ: Prentice Hall, 1970.

Kailin, Jesse. "On Ethical Egoism." *American Philosophical Quarterly, Monograph Series No. 1. Studies in Moral Philosophy* (1968): 26-41.

Krebs, Dennis. "Psychological Approaches to Altruism: An Evaluation." *Ethics* 92 (1982): 447-458.

Machan, Tibor. "Recent Works on Ethical Egoism." *American Philosophical Quarterly* 16, no. 1 (January, 1979): 1-15.

MacIntyre, Alasdair. "Egoism and Altruism." *Encyclopedia of Philosophy.* Paul Edwards, ed. New York: Macmillan, 1967.

Milo, Ronald D, ed. *Egoism and Altruism*. Belmont CA: Wadsworth, 1973.

Nagel, Thomas. *The Possibility of Altruism*. Oxford: Clarendon Press, 1986.

Plato. *The Republic*. Trans. Allan Bloom. New York: Basic Books, 1968.

Rachels, James. "Two Auguments Against Ethical Egoism." *Philosophia* 4 (1974): 297-314.

Rand, Ayn, ed. *The Virtue of Selfishness*. New York: Penguin, 1964.

Regis, Edward. "What is Ethical Egoism?" *Ethics* 91 (October 1980): 50-62.

Shaver, Robert William. *Rational Egoism*. New York: Cambridge University Press, 1998.

Singer, Peter. *The Expanding Circle*. New York: Ferrar, Straus and Giroux, 1981.

Sober, Elliot. "What is Psychological Egoism?" *Behaviorism* 17 (1989): 89-102.

chapter 7

UTILITARIANISM

Case Study: Hottie or Nottie

Mildred Schlossberg is a sophomore at Springfield University. For the past two years she has shared a dorm room with her best friend, Carmella Pio. The two have known each other since elementary school and are about as close as two people can get.

About six months ago, Carmella's boyfriend of two years, Vinny Cheramonte, broke up with her suddenly, saying that their relationship had been stale for some time. Because Vinny is considered a highly desirable boyfriend — "he's like sooo cool, has a great sense of humor and a really hot bod"—Carmella became extremely depressed after the breakup and has refused to talk about Vinny with anyone, even Mildred.

Two weeks ago Mildred bumped into Vinny in a local student bar and the two began an intense, highly passionate relationship. Mildred realized that she had always had strong feelings for Vinny, but could never act on them because he was in a relationship with her best friend. After several incredible dates, she is beginning to think that Vinny may in fact be her soul mate—the man she is meant to be with for the rest of her life.

Now Mildred is stuck in a dilemma. She has weighed three possible courses of action that she could now take, but can't decide which one would be the best moral choice: (1) She could tell Carmella the truth about her relationship with Vinny, but she knows that this will undoubtedly cause her pain, since she still has feelings for her former flame. Telling the truth might also cause Carmella to feel that Mildred has betrayed her, thus putting their relationship into jeopardy. (2) She could continue to sneak around with Vinny until Carmella has gotten over her feelings of rejection and then tell her the truth when she would be more receptive to hearing about it. The problem here is that Carmella might find out what is going on and really be devastated. (3) She could break off her relationship with Vinny in order not to cause her friend pain, but then she would be sacrificing what could potentially be one of the most meaningful relationships she has ever had.

> **For Discussion**
>
> What would an ethical egoist advise Mildred to do? Imagine that Mildred was recommended by a friend to consider the impact that her decision would have on all those who are affected by her potential actions. Who are all the people involved in this case and what are the positive and negative consequences that each of the choices that she is considering would have on these people? Based upon this consideration, what is the right thing for Mildred to do?

Utilitarianism, like ethical egoism, is a consequentialist moral theory—that is, a theory in which the goodness or badness of an act is determined exclusively by the consequences of that act. The ethical egoist, as we've seen, is concerned only with producing the best possible outcome for him or herself. Utilitarians, however, broaden the sphere of moral concern to include **all** those who are affected by a given act. All utilitarians follow what has come to be known as the "principle of utility." This principle states that:

> *Everyone ought to act so as to bring about the greatest amount of good, or happiness, for all those who are affected by the act.*

In utilitarianism, the good of everyone is considered equally important, and no one—oneself included—counts any more or less than anyone else. Thus when the good of the majority outweighs your own good, a utilitarian would argue that you are obligated to act in the majority's interest, even if this means sacrificing your own. In this sense utilitarianism avoids the pitfalls of ethical egoism, which gives exclusive concern to one's own good.

From the case study at the beginning of this chapter, you probably now realize that, if Mildred was simply concerned only with her own well-being when deciding whether or not to date Vinny, she would be operating out of an ethical egoist moral framework. But what if she decided to take others into consideration who might be affected by her actions? She'd still be a consequentialist, because all she's considering when determining whether her action is right or wrong are the consequences or effects of that action. But now she's moving from an ethical egoist moral framework to a more utilitarian one. Her own well-being would still be important in her moral calculations, but so too would be the well-being of other people who are affected by her actions.

Needless to say, utilitarianism is a somewhat more complex moral system than ethical egoism: it's always more difficult to think about the needs of others rather than simply looking out for one's own interests. There are those who believe, however, that utilitarianism provides a more nuanced and complete perspective on moral action than is possible using ethical egoist principles.

Before we can assess the worth of utilitarianism as a moral theory, however, the theory first has to be explained. And this requires a brief but necessary exploration of the historical development of utilitarian theory.

Classic Utilitarianism: Bentham and Mill

The origins of utilitarian theory can be found in the writing of the English social reformers, Jeremy Bentham (1748-1832) and John Stuart Mill (1806-1832). Bentham and Mill were determined to change what they perceived to be the corrupt laws and social practices of their day. British society in the late 18th century was already beginning to stratify into a world of have and have-nots. As Charles Dickens would later describe so well in novels such as *Oliver Twist,* conditions among the poor in English society were horrific, with harsh penalties for those who fell into debt and no child labor laws in existence.

Jeremy Bentham was dismayed by the plight of his fellow citizens and was motivated to develop a moral principle that, if applied, he believed would greatly help improve their lot in life. This principle— the principle of utility—would become the starting point for utilitarian ethics, with Bentham establishing as a "fundamental axiom" that "the greatest happiness of the greatest number that is the measure of right and wrong." (*Fragment,* preface).

In his major work, *Introduction to the Principles of Morals and Legislation,* Bentham defines happiness in a purely hedonistic way as the experience of a greater amount of pleasure than pain. Pleasure for Bentham is the only intrinsic good—that is the only thing that is good in itself. All other things we consider good (fame, fortune, freedom, etc.) are instrumental goods: they are useful, in other words, because they can help us to attain pleasure.

Being a product of his age, Bentham believed it possible to come up with a scientific way to measure quantities of pleasure and pain produced by a given act. In particular, he thought it necessary to measure each of the following features of the pleasure and pain produced:

1. *intensity*: how strong or weak is it?
2. *duration:* how long will it last?
3. *certainty*: what is the probability that it will occur?
4. *propinquity:* how soon will it be fulfilled?
5. *fecundity:* what is the probability that it will be followed by a similar pleasure or pain?
6. *purity*: what is the probability that it will be followed by the opposite sensation (e.g., pain after pleasure)?
7. *extent*: how many people will be affected?

Bentham believed that if we could just quantify the amount of pleasure produced by an act, the "hedonic calculus" that resulted would serve as an exact guide for moral reasoning.

Here's how Bentham thought his hedonic calculus would work: First, we sum up all the pleasures produced by a given act. The value of each pleasure would be determined by applying each of the seven features described above, and the sum of each would be added together. We would engage in the same process for each of the pains produced. The negatives would be subtracted from the positives to determine if the act was more pleasurable than painful for all those affected. If that's the case, the act would be considered morally correct and should be carried out; if not it would be considered morally wrong.

Bentham restricted his hedonic calculus only to the seven aspects of pleasure mentioned above. His concern therefore was purely about the quantity of pleasure produced, not the quality of the pleasure. No pleasure, he believed, was intrinsically higher or lower, better or worse, than any other: there was no qualitative difference between the pleasure produced by a night at the opera or that produced by drinking gin at a dingy bar. The reason for Bentham's hesitation to introduce the concept of qualitative differences between different pleasurable acts is that the idea of quality would introduce a subjective element into his system that would destroy his attempts to create a "moral arithmetic." As he was quoted as saying by Mill, "quality of pleasure being equal, pushpin [a simple English table game] is as good as poetry." (Mill, "Bentham" 123). It was statements like these the led critics like the historian Thomas Carlyle to derided Bentham's approach to ethics as "pig philosophy" because of its emphasis on bodily pleasures.

It was left to another generation of utilitarian thinkers to attempt to salvage Bentham's theory from criticisms like these. John Stuart Mill was actually Bentham's godson and raised by his father according to Benthamite principles. Like Bentham, Mill was an ardent social reformer, who wrote works in favor of personal liberty (*On Liberty*) and the right of women to vote (*On the Subjugation of Women*). Mill's aim was to take Bentham's utilitarian system and make it better suited to the "modern" world of 19th century England.

Mill completely accepted the starting point of Bentham's philosophy that "actions are right in proportion as they tend to promote happiness, wrong as they tend to produce the reverse of happiness. By happiness is intended pleasure, and the absence of pain; by unhappiness, pain, and the privation of pleasure."

Where Mill differed from Bentham was in the fact that he was more than willing to consider qualitative aspects of pleasure in his own approach to utilitarianism. Mill argued that there were higher and lower pleasures and the higher pleasures were preferable to the lower. As Mill puts it, "It is better to be a human being dissatisfied than a pig satisfied; better to be a Socrates dissatisfied than a fool satisfied. And if the fool or the pig, are of a different opinion, it is only because they only know their own side of the question" (*Utilitarianism*). For Mill, lower pleasures (pig pleasures) were sensual or bodily pleasures; higher pleasures (Socrates' pleasures) were pleasures of the intellect.

Mill then goes on to give his justification for the claim that higher pleasures are superior to lower ones, using what has come to be referred to as the "competent judge test." If we want to know, he says, the relative qualities of two different pleasures, we need to seek out those who are "competently acquainted with both" to rank them:

> Of two pleasures, if there be one to which all or almost all who have experienced both give a decided preference, irrespective of a feeling of moral obligation to prefer it, that is the more desirable pleasure. Now it is an unquestionable fact that those who are equally acquainted with and equally capable of appreciating and enjoying both [physical and intellectual pleasures] do give a most marked preference to the manner of existence which employs their higher faculties. Few human creatures would consent to be changed into any of the lower animals for a promise of the fullest allowance of a beast's pleasures; no intelligent human being would consent to be a fool, no instructed person would be an ignoramus, no person of feeling and conscience would be

selfish and base, even though they should be persuaded that the fool, the dunce, or the rascal is better satisfied with his lot than they are with theirs (Utilitarianism).

Mill argues that those individuals of high mental ability who have experienced both pleasures of the physical and intellectual variety give the preference to intellectual pleasures, ranking them as superior. On the other hand, those of limited mental capacity are unable of experiencing the higher pleasures of the mind, and therefore are not capable of passing adequate judgment on the relative qualities of each.

There are numerous difficulties with Mill's position on the superiority of intellectual pleasure—not the least of which being that his reasoning is both circular and somewhat elitist. Certainly, the majority can often be wrong about many things (as Mill himself pointed out in *On Liberty*). There is also the problem of what constitutes a qualified judge. Finally, it isn't necessarily true that most people—or even highly refined people— would choose higher pleasures (going to an art gallery) over lower ones (having sex or eating a good meal) if they had the choice. It would seem that, in his attempt to save utilitarian theory from the criticism of being little more than "pig philosophy" by introducing the concept of higher and lower pleasures, Mill has unintentionally introduced even more difficulties into the theory.

Despite these criticisms, Mill's achievement was to recognize that an existence devoted simply to physical pleasure would be a greatly diminished sort of human life. It seems intuitively true that a complete life would include both lower and higher sorts of pleasures: sex, drink, and rock and roll—to be sure—but also poetry, art, great music, and philosophy. And a life devoid of the latter clearly would be a life that is less than fully human. Notwithstanding Mill's ability to offer a strong argument in defense of his addition of qualitative dimensions of pleasure, then, we still might agree with him that in the end it is indeed preferable to be a dissatisfied Socrates than a satisfied pig.

Act Utilitarianism

In the 20th century, utilitarian theory came to take on two main forms— act utilitarianism and rule utilitarianism. The basic difference between these two is that an act utilitarian would apply the principle of utility to specific actions, while the rule utilitarian applies this principle to moral rules.

The approach that Bentham and Mill took was clearly that of act utilitarianism. In this approach, for each individual act we are about to perform, we need to appeal directly to the principle of utility—that is, we must ask ourselves whether this specific act in this circumstance will produce the greatest amount of good (or the greatest happiness) for all those involved. We do this by weighing the positive and negative consequences of an action. If the act produces a greater amount of good than evil for all those who are affected by the act, then the act is good; if not, the act is bad.

Moral Decision-Making Using Act Utilitarianism

Step 1: Determine who will be affected by this action.

Step 2: Analyze all the possible consequences (short- and long-term, direct and indirect) of the action for all those who are affected.

Step 3: Determine if the action, more than any other alternative available at the time, will produce the greatest amount of good, or happiness, for all those affected by the action.

Step 4: If it does, then the act is morally right; if it doesn't then the act is morally wrong.

But what about moral rules that are commonly accepted, such as "don't lie"? Can't rules like these be used as a guide for one's actions? According to John Stuart Mill, such rules, while in general appropriate to follow, cannot be used as an absolute guide in moral decision-making. There are many instances when lying, in fact, may be perfectly acceptable—for example, when telling the truth will subject an innocent to a greater evil. The individual who lies to thugs about where their victim is hiding is also probably behaving properly even though he is forced to resort to a deception. Mill's point is that while relying on moral rules may be helpful at times, when following those rules causes more harm than good, we should not hesitate to discard them.

Advantages of Act Utilitarianism

As we have seen, the utilitarian approach is certainly to be credited for the attempt it makes to look beyond the individual's own interest in determining which actions are right and wrong. Any legitimate utilitarian must always be concerned with how his actions affect others, his own well-being weighing no more heavily than any other's in determining which actions he should or should not perform. "The happiness which forms the utilitarian standard of what is right in conduct, is not the agent's own happiness," writes Mill, "but that of all concerned. As between his own happiness and that of others, utilitarianism requires him to be as strictly impartial as a disinterested and benevolent spectator."

As we have seen, in certain circumstances a utilitarian may even be obligated to sacrifice his own happiness and well-being if doing so will help to promote the greater good. In this sense, utilitarianism represents a marked improvement over approaches which make self-interest the basis for ethical decision making, and is certainly preferable to moral subjectivism insofar as it provides some kind of objective standard of right and wrong.

Disadvantages of Act Utilitarianism

For all of its advantages as a moral system, there are some serious problems with act utilitarianism that must be considered:

Act utilitarianism is an impractical approach to decision-making. One obvious problem with act utilitarianism is that it seems like an impractical approach for helping to guide one in moral decision-making. For one thing, although a person may be able to gauge the direct and immediate effects of his action, it is considerably more difficult to gauge the indirect and long-term effects. Indeed one might argue that it is in fact impossible to calculate every possible consequence of an action. An act might very well produce positive benefits initially, but in the long run might prove extremely harmful. A second problem with act utilitarianism is that when an individual is faced with a moral dilemma, he is often required to make instantaneous decisions. If he has to weigh the positive and negative effects of each action that he is about to perform, and also consider long-term effects, he will ultimately be paralyzed. Therefore if we are to be able to make useful moral decisions, we need to have some clear and concrete rules that can be appealed to in various circumstances.

Act utilitarianism can lead to violations of the rights of individuals and minority groups. For example, suppose a utilitarian has to decide whether or not painful scientific studies on orphaned mentally retarded children ought to be performed. He is convinced that these experiments could realistically lead to a cure that could save thousands of "normal" children in the future. This kind of experimentation could easily be justified by engaging in a utilitarian calculus. The experiments would not cause mental pain to others because the children are orphaned, and their disability—assuming that it is severe enough—would prevent them from having the kind of mental anguish that many of us would have knowing we were about to be experimented on against our wills. If unfortunate accidents did occur as a result of the experimentation that cut short the lives of these children, at least the experimenters would have the satisfaction of knowing that the future prospects of these children were dim anyway, and, had they lived, they would only have been a drain on the resources of society. Consequently, our utilitarian researcher should have no qualms about performing these experiments, even though such practices would be rejected completely by most civilized people.

Peter Singer, a prominent utilitarian thinker, goes even further than this when he maintains that if we indeed had to perform such experiments, it would be preferable to do so on severely mentally handicapped orphans than on healthy rats. The rats, he says, would be "more intelligent, more aware of what is happening to them, more sensitive to pain, and so on, than many severely brain damaged humans barely surviving in hospital wards and other institutions." (*Practical Ethics*, 67-68).

Act utilitarianism can lead to violations of the basic principles of justice. An act utilitarian approach can also easily be used to violate the principles of justice. The most basic demands of justice state that we treat people fairly and reward or punish them based upon their own merits. As the following imaginary case illustrates, it is all too easy to violate this principle using a utilitarian approach:

> Suppose a utilitarian were visiting an area in which there was racial strife, and that, during his visit, a Negro rapes a white woman, and that race riots occur as a result of the crime, white mobs, with the connivance of the police, bashing and killing Negroes, etc. Suppose too that our utilitarian is in the area of the crime when it is committed such that his testimony would bring about the conviction of a particular Negro. If he knows that a quick arrest will stop the riots and lynching, surely, as a utilitarian, he must conclude that he has a duty to bear false witness in order to bring about the punishment of an innocent person (McCloskey, 239-255).

A utilitarian in this position would have to support the idea of bearing false witness against an innocent man. Weighing his options, he would certainly realize that the benefits of a return to public order far outweighs the need to protect the life of one innocent human being.

An Alternative: Rule Utilitarianism

The other form that utilitarian theory takes is known as rule utilitarianism. According to this approach, certain moral rules, if followed, will always produce the greatest amount of good over evil. Thus a rule utilitarian would maintain that, instead of each individual acting to bring about the greatest amount of good over evil, everyone should follow those rules which will tend to bring about the greatest amount of good. The basic principle that a rule utilitarian would follow, therefore, would be a slightly modified version of the principle of utility:

> *Everyone ought to act from those moral rules, the following of which would bring about greatest amount of good, or happiness, for all those affected by the action.*

For example, instead of wondering in each and every moral situation whether one ought to tell the truth or not, one would establish a rule like the following: "one should always tell the truth because doing so will produce the greater good." Certainly it might be the case that in a specific situation telling the truth will not produce good consequences (for example, telling one's already depressed grandfather that he has only six months to live), but in general, the rule utilitarian would argue that it is in the best interest of society if everyone told the truth. Similarly, a rule utilitarian would argue that following a rule like "always keep your promises" would produce the greatest amount of good over evil within a society. Therefore, unless there is some legitimate reason for not keeping your promises (e.g., you are caught up in an emergency situation), you ought always to do so. Other rules that a rule utilitarian might support might be something like: "Do not kill except in self-defense" (or the similar rule: "Do not kill innocents"), "Do not cheat," and "Always protect innocent human life."

Moral Decision-Making Using Rule Utilitarianism

Preparation: Select a limited number of rules, which, if followed, will generally achieve the greatest amount of good, or happiness, for all those who are affected by the act. You may want to write these rules down, so you remember them.

Step 1: Determine who will be affected by this action.
Step 2: Assess what moral rules apply to the action that you are considering.
Step 3: Determine if the action being considered accords with these moral rules.
Step 4: If it does, then the act is morally right; if it doesn't then the act is morally wrong.

There are certain definite advantages that rule utilitarianism has over its counterpart. For one thing, rule utilitarianism makes moral decision-making less complex than act utilitarianism. Instead of having to decide in every specific circumstance whether an act is producing the greatest good for the greatest number, one only needs to appeal to a rule that will achieve this same result. This inevitably speeds up moral decision-making. It is also true that the theory manages to avoid the dubious sorts of moral difficulties associated with act utilitarianism that we have discussed above. By following rules like "Do not kill innocents," or "Do not cheat," it is unlikely that a rule utilitarian would engage in the kinds of odious practices that could be condoned using act utilitarianism.

Despite some of the advantages of rule utilitarianism, there are definite problems with the theory that are difficult to overcome. First, *it is not so easy to find rules that do not admit of any exceptions.* Thiroux uses the example of the rule, "Never kill except in self-defense," which would seem to be the kind of rule that would appeal to a rule utilitarian. But even this rule would seem to admit certain exceptions:

> can the rule never kill except in self-defense actually cover all situations human beings will become involved in? Will it cover abortion, for example? Many antiabortionists think so, stating that in no way can the unborn fetus be considered an aggressor; therefore, it cannot be aborted. Prochoice advocates, on the other hand, either don't consider the fetus a human being or argue for the precedence of the mother's life over the fetus's and believe that there are times when the fetus must be aborted. How, for example, would the rule utilitarian deal with aborting the fetus when the mother's life is endangered not specifically because she is pregnant but for some other reason? The fetus cannot be considered the aggressor, so how can it be aborted in self-defense? (51)

There is also the problem that *moral rules can often come into conflict with one another.* What happens for example when the rule, "Tell the truth," comes into conflict with the rule, "Protect innocent human life." Which rule should we follow? Unfortunately, rule utilitarianism has no way of deciding between conflicting rules, except by reverting back to act utilitarianism.

Finally, *rule utilitarianism seems to contradict itself* by at the same time seeming to both accept and reject the principle of utility—the bedrock of utilitarian theory. If the goal in our moral actions is to strive to produce a maximum balance of good over evil, as all utilitarians hold, then one may have to allow for the same kinds of problematic actions, including punishing the innocent, that made act utilitarianism seem so morally repugnant. If on the other hand, rules calling for truth telling at all times or protecting the innocent are followed, then it must be recognized that at times the principle of utility will have to be sacrificed.

For Further Discussion

1. Return to Exercise #1 on page 87 in the chapter on ethical egoism. Applying the principle of utility, assess whether the actions descibed would be considered right or wrong.

2. Utilitarianism and Public Policy: Very often public policy decisions in the United States are made by adopting a utilitarian calculus. When determining whether or not to adopt specific legislation, elected officials will often look to see if the greatest good for the greatest number will be achieved if the legislation is enacted. Imagine that you are a new member of Congress, and are trying to determine whether or not the following policies should be enacted. You are also a scrupulous utilitarian, so your decision should be based exclusively on the principle of utility:

    • In order to stem the rising tide of teen crime, all individuals under the age of 21 will hereby be subject to a curfew that requires them to be off the streets by 10pm.

    • In order to promote a healthy sense of citizenship, upon graduating from high school all Americans will hereby be obligated to perform two years of social service or one year of military service.

    • In order to encourage voting, a law will be enacted fining American citizens $100 for failure to vote in any November election.

- In order to curb emissions that contribute to global-warming, a new tax will be placed upon gasoline, raising the price in the New York area to $7.00 a gallon.

- In order to reduce health care costs for everyone and to promote good health, it will now be permitted for insurance companies to charge cigarette smokers and obese individuals with an insurance premium significant enough to off-set the costs that such individuals add to health care because of their unhealthy lifestyles.

Sources and Further Reading

Albee, Ernest. *A History of English Utilitarianism*, New York: Routledge, 2004.

Bentham, Jeremy. "Fragment on Government." *The Works of Jeremy Bentham*. Vol. 1. Ed. John Bowering. Edinburgh:

—. *The Introduction to the Principles of Morals and Legislation*. Ed. J.H. Burns and H.L.A. Hart. London: Athline Press, 1970.

Crisp, Roger. *Routledge Philosophy Guidebook to Mill on Utilitarianism*. London: Routledge, 1997.

Feinberg, Joel. "The Forms and Limits of Utilitarianism." *Philosophical Review* 76 (1967): 368-381.

Glover, Jonathan. *Utilitarianism and Its Critics*. New York: Macmillan, 1990.

Lyons, David. "Utilitarianism." *Encyclopedia of Ethics*. Eds. Lawrence C. Becker and Charlotte B. Becker. New York: Garland, 1992.

McCloskey, H.J. "A Non-Utilitarian Approach to Punishment." *Inquiry* 8 (1965).

Mill, John Stuart. "Bentham." *Utilitarianism, On Liberty, and Essay on Bentham*. Ed. M. Warnock. New York: New American Library, 1974.

—. *Utilitarianism*. Indianapolis: Bobbs-Merrill, 1957.

Pettit, Philip. "Consequentialism." *A Companion to Ethics*. Ed. Peter Singer. Oxford Blackwell, 1991.

Scarre, Geoffrey. *Utilitarianism*. London: Routledge, 1996.

Scheffler, Samuel. *The Rejection of Consequentialism*. Oxford: Clarendon Press, 1982.

Sheng, C.L. *Defense of Utilitarianism*. Lanham, MD: University Press of America, 2004.

Singer, Peter. *The Expanding Circle*. New York: Ferrar, Straus and Giroux, 1981.

—. *Practical Ethics*. Cambridge: Cambridge University Press, 1993.

Smart, J.J.C. and Williams, Bernard. *Utilitarianism: For and Against*. Cambridge: Cambridge University Press, 1987.

Smith, James M. and Sosa, Ernest, eds. *Mill's Utilitarianism: Text and Criticism*. Belmont, CA: Wadsworth, 1969.

chapter

DEONTOLOGY

Case Study: Constructing a Moral Dilemma

Tony DeStefano is a part-time student majoring in political science at St. Ignatius College in Baltimore. Because his parents are fairly poor, Tony has to pay for college classes completely on his own. He eventually hopes to go to law school, but at the rate he is going, it will take him almost seven years just to graduate from college.

To help pay his tuition, Tony has been working during the day at Zaffuto Construction Company, one of the largest, most respected, and most profitable construction companies in Baltimore. Mr. Zaffuto, the owner of the company, is a major player in the world of Baltimore politics and, because of his connections, receives millions of dollars in construction contracts every year from the city.

Mr. Zaffuto, who thinks extremely highly of Tony, would like nothing more than to see him finish law school and make a success of his life. One day he calls Tony into his office and takes him into his confidence. Mr. Zaffuto tells Tony that building materials that are supposed to be used for city projects are often stolen at night and have to be replaced at the city's expenses. He says that this is not unusual in the construction profession and that no one in city government thinks twice about it. He then reveals to Tony that he in fact is the one taking these materials and using them for his own private construction projects—a scheme which nets him several million dollars a year. This has been going on for over twenty years, he says, and because most of the major politicians and law enforcement officials in Baltimore are on his "payroll," there is no danger of getting caught.

Mr. Zaffuto then tells Tony that he needs someone that he can trust to help load these materials onto his trucks at night, so that they can "disappear" from the construction site. He also tells Tony that he is willing to give him a cut of $30,000 for his labors, which is more than enough to pay for his full-time tuition at the college and still save a substantial *amount for law school. Best of all, he would only need to work one night a week, and so he can devote most of his time to his studies.*

For Discussion

What would an ethical egoist advise Tony to do in this situation? A utilitarian? Imagine that it is true that Tony would never get caught moving the construction supplies and that this scheme would in fact solve all of his financial difficulties. Is it still wrong for Tony to take Mr. Zaffuto up on his offer? If so, why?

Having examined two consequentialist ethical theories—ethical egoism and utilitarianism—we can now turn our attention to a few notable non-consequentialist theories. As we have already seen, non-consequentialist theories reject the idea that the goodness or badness of an act can be determined by its consequences. Instead, they argue that there must be something intrinsic to the act itself which makes it right or wrong.

One of the most famous of these nonconsequentialist theories goes by the name deontology. The word deontology actually comes from the Greek, *deon*, meaning duty. If you do your duty, you are doing what is right for its own sake and not because of any benefit derived from it. Deontology, therefore, offers an interesting counterpoint to theories such as ethical egoism and utilitarianism, which are exclusively consequence-driven theories.

Let's use cheating to illustrate the differences between these two approaches. The utilitarian would argue that the act of cheating could be morally acceptable if this act produces a greater balance of good over evil. Most of us, however, intuitively recognize that there is something morally wrong with cheating no matter what kind of positive consequences such an act produces. But what is it about cheating that makes it wrong? The deontologist would argue that there is something inherent in the act itself that determines whether it is right or wrong, regardless of the consequences. For a deontologist

an act is right if, and only if, it accords with a rule that can be universalized.

Although there are several possible rules that a deontologist might cite as the basis for moral decision- making, two stand out as being the most common: the golden rule and the principle of respect for persons.

The Golden Rule

Imagine the following situation: As you approach a railroad crossing, you notice a car has stopped on the tracks and the occupant, an elderly woman, is unconscious in the car. A train is rapidly approaching and has no time to stop before it crashes into the car. You have to decide what to do. If you jump out of your own car and try to save the woman, you yourself might be killed. If you were an ethical egoist, you would consider it foolish to risk your own life to save this woman. If you were a utilitarian, you would also probably not help her, because the greater good is not served by risking your life for someone who may not have many years to live anyway.

With little hesitation, however, you rush to the car and pull out the woman with only a few seconds to spare before it is destroyed by the on-coming train. Later, when you are asked why you risked your own life to save a mere stranger, you cite a basic moral rule that you have spent your life attempting to follow: "Do unto others as you would have them do unto you." In risking your own life, you were following what has come to be known as "the golden rule." Although you may know this rule from its Christian form, in fact many of the major religious traditions of the world have some version or other of the golden rule.

Most parents raise their children to follow this basic rule without even realizing it. For example, when a child does something wrong, his parents will typically not ask him if his actions produced positive benefits for himself or others. They will usually say something along the lines of "how would you like it if someone did that to you?"

Moral Decision-Making Using the Golden Rule

Step 1: Identify the act being considered.
Step 2: Determine whether it accords with a rule that can be universalized—in this case, the golden rule.
Step 3: If it does, then the act is right; if it doesn't, then the act is wrong.

Kant's Categorical Imperative

The most important attempt to construct a deontological approach to ethics is found in the moral writing of Emmanual Kant (1724-1804). Kant was a professor at the University of Konigsberg in Prussia and is considered one of the "greats" in the history of philosophy. His *Groundwork of the Metaphysics of Morals*, though brief in length, is acknowledged to be one of the great achievements of enlightenment thought. It is to this work that we will now turn in order to consider Kant's unique contribution to moral thought.

In the *Groundwork*, Kant rejects the basic premise of utilitarianism—namely, that consequences alone determine whether an act is right or wrong. Kant believes that consequences, in fact, are irrelevant in determining the moral status of an action. For example, if we could save many lives by sacrificing one innocent person, the act would still be intrinsically wrong for Kant, despite any positive benefits that the act might produce.

Kant also rejects utilitarianism because he believes that the consequences of our actions are often beyond our control, and, therefore, we should not be held responsible for them. Imagine that you are walking down the street and you see someone dying of a heart attack. You stop to help the person using CPR, but accidentally kill him in the process. Kant would argue that in performing this beneficent act you did the right thing and should not be held responsible for the unintended outcome of your action. Though the results of your action may have been unfortunate, you did not behave immorally.

Kant argues that the truly moral person is one who acts solely for the sake of duty—that is, out of a concern and respect for the moral law. But how do we know where our duty lies? The answer, says Kant, is that our duty lies in obedience to a particular rule, principle, or law regardless of inclination, self-interest, or consequences. It lies, in other words, in following a command that must be obeyed for its own sake. Kant calls this supreme principle of all morality the *categorical imperative*.

An imperative is nothing more than a command. In order to understand what Kant means by a categorical imperative, it must be contrasted with what he refers to as a hypothetical imperative. A hypothetical imperative is conditional: it tells you what you ought to do if you want to achieve a certain result. This kind of imperative has the form, "Do X to achieve Y." For example: "If you want to do well in your college classes, then make sure you study every night." This specific hypothetical imperative tells you what to do if you want to succeed in college. Of course, if you have no interest in succeeding in college, you don't need to follow such an imperative.

Kant, however, believed that moral obligations take on a very different form than most of the other obligations we have in life. If there is something that I am morally obligated to do, then I ought to do it no matter what. All moral obligations, then, take on the form of categorical imperatives. They always take the form, "Do X" (e.g., "Tell the truth."). Such moral obligations are unconditional (they apply no matter what) and universally binding (they apply not just to me but to everyone).

We have already seen that for a utilitarian the principle of utility is the basic tool for determining in every situation whether an act is right or wrong. Kant uses the categorical imperative for a similar purpose. It is his yardstick for determining right and wrong. Although Kant developed at least four different formulations of the categorical imperative, we will focus on his two most famous versions of this principle—the principle of universalizability and the principle of respect for persons.

The Principle of Universalizability

The first formulation of this Categorical Imperative is: "I ought never to act except in such a way that my maxim should become a universal law" (Kant 70). For each act that I am planning to perform, then, I have to ask:

1. What is the rule authorizing this act that I am about to perform? and
2. Can it become a universal rule for all human beings to follow?

Thus an act would be considered immoral for Kant if the rule that would authorize it (the maxim) cannot be universalized—that is, turned into a general rule for all to follow. To put this in another way, if we cannot affirm that everyone ought to act in the same way that we have done, we know our action is wrong.

Two examples would help to illustrate how Kant's system works. In the first example, Johnny Scollazo borrows money from a friend and promises to pay it back, although he has no intention to do so. Having some conscience he wonders if such an act is morally correct. Remembering what he learned about Kant in his college ethics class, he turns this into a rule, "Whenever I am short of money, I will borrow money and promise to pay it back, although I know that I will never do so." He then turns his rule into a universal law to see if it is right. What would happen, he wonders, if everyone broke their promises to repay money? The answer is that no one would ever lend money to anyone else, because they would never trust anyone's promises to repay the money they borrowed. Johnny immediately realizes that his act cannot be universalized without contradiction, and therefore it is not right.

In the second example, Eddie Dougherty, a lazy fellow, who is not really interested in working, is thinking of stealing from others to get what he wants. The rule for the action he is considering would be something like the following: "I shall never work but steal from other human beings." If this rule were universalized it would become: "no human beings should ever work but should steal what they need from each other." The reason why this rule cannot be universalized is fairly apparent: if no one worked, there would be no one to steal from and nothing to steal. Thus Kant would say that the action that Eddie is contemplating is immoral because it cannot be universalized without contradiction.

The Principle of Respect for Persons

The second formulation of the categorical imperative goes as follows:

> Always treat humanity, whether in your own person or that of another, never merely as a means, but always at the same time as an end.

In the *Foundations of the Metaphysics of Morals*, Kant goes on to elaborate:

> Man regarded as a *person*...is exalted above any price; for as a person...he is not to be valued merely as a means to the ends of others..., but as an end in himself, that is, he possesses a *dignity* (an absolute inner worth) by which he exacts *respect* from himself and from all other rational beings in the world. He can measure himself with any other being of his kind and value himself on a footing of equality with them (230).

Unlike animals and other living things, human beings have a special status conferred upon them because they possess rationality. Kant's principle of respect for persons tells us to treat other human beings always *as ends in themselves*—that is, as persons having intrinsic worth. To treat someone as having intrinsic worth is to recognize in all of our dealings with them that they have value in themselves as rational agents.

Let's make things clear here: Kant is definitely not saying that we can never use another person as a means to achieve our own purposes. It would be extremely difficult to live in the world in which we do without using people as means at least some of the time. For example, every time we go to a store, we are using the cashier as a means to purchase products that we need. According to Kant, this is perfectly fine as long as the cashier is acting autonomously in serving us.

What the principle of respect for persons states is that we can never use another human being *merely* as a means to our own ends. When we use someone merely as a means we are involving them in a scheme of action to which they could not in principle give consent. When we manipulate, coerce or deceive someone into doing something for us, then we are using them merely as a means, and this, according to Kant, is always wrong.

Moral Decision-Making Using Kant's Categorical Imperative

Step 1: Identify the act being considered.
Step 2: Determine whether it accords with a rule that can be universalized.
Step 3: If it does, then the act is right; if it doesn't, then the act is wrong.

Putting Kant's theory of respect for persons into practice is at times more difficult than relying on egoist or utilitarian approaches, which focus solely on consequences. We must always recognize that other human beings have their own goals, aims, and projects and we must strive to respect these. This is the reason why Kant believes deceiving someone is morally wrong, even when we think that we are doing so for his or her own good. This can lead to some unpleasant situations with friends or coworkers who may not always appreciate the value of candor.

The principle of respect for persons also demands that we allow competent adults to make their own decisions in life, even when we may not agree with their decisions. This becomes particularly tricky when we are faced with a mentally competent adult who decides to commit suicide. While Kant himself thought suicide was wrong, the principle of respect for persons would seem to demand that we respect the autonomy of the rational person who seeks to end his or her own life for whatever reason.

Kant and The Problem of Lying

A close friend of yours who is "generously proportioned" has been trying to lose weight for several months with only modest success. When she sees you she asks if you can tell that she has lost weight. You, however, don't notice any difference at all in her size. Should you be perfectly honest with your friend, and tell her that she looks exactly the same to you? Or, in this particular case, might it not be acceptable for the sake of your friend's psychological well-being to misrepresent the truth just a little bit?

We know how a utilitarian in this situation might respond. Applying the principle of utility, he would ask which possible course of action would produce the best possible consequences for all those who are affected by the act. Those affected in this case only include himself and his overweight friend. A utilitarian might very well choose to lie to a friend, since it would serve his own good (avoid the unpleasant effects of a truthful comment) as well as that of his friend (who would be encouraged to continue her diet program).

But how would a deontologist deal with this same situation? Kant, as we would expect, has a fairly rigid position against lying. He uses one of the most extreme situations imaginable to make his case. Imagine, he says, that a man fleeing from a murderer asks to hide in your house. The murderer comes along and asks you where the man went. You know that if you tell the truth, the man hiding will likely be killed. What should you do? For Kant the answer is clear: You have to tell the truth in all circumstances, including this one. If we lie and tell the murderer that the man whom he is chasing is not in the house, because we are afraid of what the consequences might be for telling the truth, then we are responsible for all the consequences of our action. The man that we are trying to protect might have decided to escape form the house using the back door, and by telling the lie, we put him directly in the hand of his murderer. We become complicit then in his murder. On the other hand, if we acknowledge that we can never know the consequences of our actions and follow universal principles of action in all circumstances, then we are on much firmer ground morally speaking, according to Kant (see "The Supposed Right to Lie from Benevolent Motives" in Part 3 of this work).

This does not mean that Kant, following his principle of respect for persons, would have absolutely no recourse but to tell the murderer exactly where his victim is hiding. Michael Sandel makes the case that Kantian deontology would allow for "hairsplitting" in a situation like this one. Hairsplitting is using a technically true but misleading statement to avoid those situations in which the unvarnished truth would cause harm, embarrassment, or social awkwardness. In the case of the overweight friend described above, an outright lie—unacceptable from Kant's perspective—would be to claim to have noticed the weight loss; the complete truth, on the other hand, might wound your friend and perhaps derail her weight-loss efforts. But one could instead say something misleading, but technically true like, "I can see that you've been trying hard to lose weight, and I'm very proud of you." No lie has been told, and the requirements of truthfulness have been satisfied.

Sandel argues that it is perfectly in keeping with Kant's approach to ethics to hairsplit when the killer asks if his victim is in the house. Avoiding both the unvarnished truth, which could cause considerable harm, and a complete lie, which would violate the principle of respect for persons, one could simply say, "I saw him down the road an hour ago," or some equally misleading but truthful statement (132-134).

Advantages of Kantian Deontology

Kant's principle of respect for person has two major benefits that have made it attractive to many moral thinkers:

Kantian Deontology is extremely egalitarian (at least when it comes to human beings). Kant's categorical imperative applies equally for all rational beings and thus avoids the problem of treating some individuals differently from others. Unfortunately non-humans are not viewed as ends in themselves and therefore have no moral standing. Although Kant may think cruelty to animals would be a bad idea because it might eventually lead us to become callous to human beings, he allows animals to be used merely as means.

Kantian Deontology cannot be used to violate individual's rights. Unlike utilitarianism, the Kantian approach, in rejecting positive consequences as the basis for moral decision-making, has a much better chance of preserving the rights of individuals and minorities than the utilitarian approach does. Indeed Kant's second formulation of the Categorical Imperative, which states that one ought never to treat any individual merely as a means but only as an end in themselves, assures that the unjust treatment of any individual, for whatever reason, must be considered wrong.

Disadvantages of Kantian Deontology

Although Kant's moral system does have some advantages over consquentialist forms of ethics such as ethical egoism and utilitarianism, as you might imagine, there are problems as well with this approach:

Kantian deontology is too rigid. As we have seen, moral rules for Kant are always absolute, bearing no exceptions. This becomes particularly problematic, as we shall see, in the example of the duty of truthfulness. Whereas each of the other moral theories that we will examine in this text are flexible enough to allow for exceptions to this duty, Kantian deontology is not, leading to some potentially problematic consequences (of course, Kant would say that he doesn't give a hoot about consequences).

The problem of conflicting duties. The example of the inquiring murderer raises another difficulty with Kant's system: namely, what to do when our moral obligations conflict with one another. As James Rachels put it, "Suppose it is held to be absolutely wrong to do A in any circumstances. Then what about the case in which a person is faced with the choice between doing A and doing B, when he must do something and no other alternatives are available?" Rachels argues that this sort of dilemma is extremely difficult to resolve if we maintain, as Kant does, that all moral rules are absolute (128).

The neglect of consequences. As we have already seen, Kant is to be congratulated for recognizing the dangers of using consequences alone as the means to determine the moral status of an act. Where he may have gone too far was in discounting the importance of consequences all together. There are many ethicists who would argue that moral intentions often have to be balanced by a consideration of consequences in order to arrive at truly moral decisions.

Ross's Deontology

Criticisms of deontology, such as those described above, led Sir William Ross (1877-1940), a Scottish philosopher, to update deontology in such a way as to soften Kant's rigid absolutism. While agreeing with Kant that consequences did not make an act right or wrong, he believed that it was necessary to take consequences into consideration when making moral choices.

Unlike Kant, Ross felt that moral duties cannot be absolute because there are certain circumstances when these duties may conflict with one another. All moral duties, therefore, are prima facie or conditional. The term prima facie literally means "at first glance," and implies that such duties, while generally morally binding, may on occasion be overridden by stronger moral claims.

In his work, *The Right and the Good* (1930), Ross identified seven prima facie duties:

1. Duties of fidelity: telling the truth, keeping actual and implied promises, and keeping contractual agreements.
2. Duties of reparation: making up for the wrongs we have done to others.
3. Duties of gratitude: recognizing what others have done for us and extending our gratitude to them.
4. Duties of justice: preventing the improper distribution of good and bad that is not in keeping with what people merit or deserve.
5. Duties of beneficence: helping to improve the condition of others in the areas of virtue, intelligence, or happiness.
6. Duties of self-improvement: the obligation we have to improve our own virtue, intelligence, and happiness.
7. Duties of nonmaleficence: not injuring others and preventing injury to others. (Thiroux, 21-22)

While acknowledging that his list of prima facie duties may be incomplete, he also maintained that all rational people would agree that these are in fact moral duties. Arguing that these prima facie duties are self-evident, Ross writes:

> I should make it plain at this stage that I am assuming the correctness of some of our main convictions as to prima facie duties, or, more strictly, am claiming that we know them to be true. To me it seems as self-evident as anything could be, that to make a promise, for instance, is to create a moral claim on us in someone else. Many readers will perhaps say that they do not know this to be true. If so, I certainly cannot prove it to them; I can only ask them to reflect again, in the hope that they will ultimately agree that they also know it to be true (22).

By acknowledging that moral duties are prima facie, Ross recognizes that they can at times come into conflict with one another. Ross attempts to solve this difficulty by providing two principles to follow in the event that prima facie duties conflict: (1) Always do that act which is in accord with the stronger prima facie duty, and (2) always do that act which has the greatest prima facie rightness over prima facie wrongness. For example, in the case of a conflict between duties of nonmaleficence and beneficence, it is obvious that our obligation not to cause harm to others outweighs any obligation to do them some positive good.

Moral Decision-Making Using Ross's Deontology

Step 1: Identify the act being considered.
Step 2: Determine whether it violates any prima facie duties.
Step 3: If it doesn't, then the act is right; if it does, then the act is wrong.

In the case where prima facie duties conflict with one another,

Step 1: Identify which duties are in conflict.
Step 2: Determine which is the stronger prima facie duty.
Step 3: An act is right if it satisfies the stronger prima facie duty; it is wrong if it satisfies the weaker duty at the expense of the stronger.

Unfortunately, Ross acknowledges that there is no set formula for determining how to apply these principles in specific circumstances. In the case of conflicting claims, he acknowledges that "while we can see with certainty that the claim exists, it becomes a matter of individual and fallible judgment to say which claim is in the circumstance the overriding one" (198). In the end we are forced to use our reason and creativity to make good moral judgments.

While Ross's version of deontology helps to correct some of the difficulties inherent in Kantian ethics, it too has some inherent difficulties. For one thing, Ross is incapable of telling us upon what basis prima facie duties are chosen. As we have seen, Ross provides a list of duties that he claims are prima facie, but provides no real justification for why these have been chosen. Most of his prima facie duties do seem intuitively valid, but this is no basis for establishing an objective moral system.

Also, Ross cannot tell us what to do when prima facie duties come into conflict with one another. Although he provides two principles, which he claims would help us to decide what to do when our prima facie duties conflict, these principles are difficult to apply. How, for example, do we determine which duty is stronger than the other?

For Further Discussion

1. Apply Kant's principle of respect for persons to each of the following cases:

   • Dr. Morty Pankoff, a highly regarded plastic surgeon, has developed a lucrative practice filling out the wrinkles in his wealthy patients faces—mainly around the lip area where facial wrinkles on middle-aged women tend to be most pronounced—using injections of fat cells. His patients think that these cells come from their own buttocks, but, in fact, Dr. Pankoff frequently uses fat cells from his own large buttock on a regular basis to save money and to spare his patients painful injections. Not realizing the source of the fat cells injected in their faces, Dr. Pankoff's patients rave about the low costs, painlessness, and wonderful results of his treatments. Based upon Kant's principle of respect for persons, what is it about this act that makes it morally wrong?

   • Adam knows that when Julie has too much to drink she loses all sense of inhibition and does things that she normally would be averse to doing. Wanting to have sexual intercourse with her, but knowing that she is not interested in him physically, Adam plans to get Julie drunk so that she will give in to his sexual advances. Since she would be technically consenting, Adam sees nothing wrong with what he is planning. Based upon Kant's principle of respect for persons, what is it about this act that makes it morally wrong?

   • You have a close friend named Mike who is extremely popular with women but also a chronic philander. In the past he has lied to numerous women about his intentions, used them for his own pleasure, and then discarded them. A few weeks ago, Mike began dating a really lovely and kind-hearted girl name Brittney, who thinks Mike really cares for her and is interested in a long-term relationship. Mike has made you promise not to reveal his history with women to any of the girls that he currently is dating, and this naturally includes Brittney. One day during a conversation, she says that she has heard some rumors about Mike's relationships with other women and asks you specifically about this. Based upon Kant's principle of respect for persons, how should you respond to Brittney's request for information about Mike?

- Sophia has been dating Brad who has a substance abuse problem. One day Sophia tells her friends that Brad has asked her to marry him. She tells her friends that she plans to marry him and says that she understands that this is risky given Brad's problems. Her friends, who believe that she is making the wrong decision and will eventually be hurt by Brad, want to convince her not to get married. Based upon the principle of respect for persons, should Sophia's friends attempt to dissuade Sophia from marrying Brad? Would your answer be the same if you applied the golden rule to this situation?

- Your four-year-old son, Eddy, is a big fan of the Christmas holidays and looks forward to that magical time when Santa delivers presents to all the good little boys and girls. In his preschool class, however, another child tells him that Santa isn't real. Eddy comes home to you extremely upset and tearfully asks you if there really is a Santa Claus. What do you think a Deontologist would advise you to do? What do you think the right thing to do in this case would be?

2. What would an ethical egoist or a utilitarian say is the morally correct thing to do in each of these cases? Would the results be dramatically different from those of a deontologist like Kant? If so, how?

Sources and Further Reading

Acton, Harry. *Kant's Moral Philosophy*. London: Macmillan, 1970.

Aune, Bruce. *Kant's Theory of Morals*. Princeton, NJ: Princeton University Press, 1979.

Augustine. *Enchiridion*. Trans. J.F. Shaw. *Nicene and Post-Nicene Fathers*. Vol. 3. Ed. Philip Schaff. Buffalo, NY: Christian Literature Publishing Company, 1887.

Darwall, Stephen. *Impartial Reason*. Ithaca, NY: Cornell University Press, 1983.

Guyer, Paul. *The Cambridge Companion to Kant.* New York: Cambridge University Press, 1992.

Kant, Immanuel. *Foundations of the Metaphysics of Morals.* Trans. Lewis White Beck. New York: Cambridge University Press, 1991.

—. "On the Supposed Right to Lie from Altruistic Motives." *Critique of Practical Reason and Other Wtitings in Moral Philosophy.* Ed. Lewis White Beck. Chicago: University of Chicago Press, 1949.

Nagel, Thomas. *The View From Nowhere.* New York: Oxford University Press, 1986.

O'Neill, Onora. *Acting on Principle: An Essay on Kantian Ethics.* New York: Columbia University Press, 1975.

Paton, Herbet J. *The Categorical Imperative: A Study in Kant's Moral Philosophy.* Chicago: University of Chicago Press, 1948.

Rachels, James. *The Elements of Moral Philosophy.* Boston: McGraw Hill, 1999.

Ross, William D. *The Right and the Good.* New York: Oxford University Press, 1930.

Sandel, Michael. *Justice.* New York: Farrar, Straus and Giroux, 2009.

Sullivan, Roger J. *Immanuel Kant's Moral Theory.* Cambridge: Cambridge University Press, 1989.

Ward, Keith. *The Development of Kant's Views on Ethics.* Oxford: Blackwell, 1972.

Wolff, Robert P. *The Anatomy of Reason: A Commentary on Kant's Groundwork of the Metaphysics of Morals.* New York: Harper and Row, 1973.

chapter 9

RIGHTS THEORY

Case Study: Free Speech or Hate Speech?

Martin Henry is a junior at Sunshine State University in Southern California. In an attempt to broaden his intellectual horizons he began reading Hitler's Mein Kampf *and similar works that advanced the theory of white supremacy. Excited about the ideas about which he had been reading, Martin decided to attend a meeting of the local chapter of Aryan Nation and soon became an active member of this organization. The members of Aryan Nation were delighted that a college student like Martin would be so committed to their cause, and even more delighted when they discovered that he was attending a liberal college like Sunshine State.*

In March 2007, Martin, at the request of the Grand Master of Aryan Nation, began to distribute fliers on his campus that informed students about the treachery of the Jewish people and argued that the Holocaust was nothing more than a myth. Although the flier didn't go so far as to advocate violence against Jews, it did maintain that past violence against this group was morally justifiable. Naturally, many students were outraged by the distribution of this flier and lodged an official complaint against Martin with the Provost of the University. After reviewing this situation, the Provost expelled Martin from Sunshine State and forbade him from ever coming onto the campus again.

Outraged by this violation of his right to freedom of speech, Martin asked the American Civil Liberties Union to defend him. Although members of this organization were disgusted by Martin's gross anti-Semitism, they agreed that his rights had in fact been violated and sued the University for two million dollars.

During the trial, Martin's lawyers argued that other controversial groups on campus, such as the Islamic Brotherhood and the Federation of Gays and Lesbians, had in the past distributed provocative materials without any disciplinary action being taken against them. Martin, they argued, was being punished because he was expressing a position that some on campus found offensive. The First Amendment, they said, was established precisely to protect people like Martin from the tyranny of majority opinion. By attempting to restrict Martin's speech—however odious it might seem—the University was posing a threat to the civil liberties of all of its students.

The lawyers for the University countered by arguing that the materials Martin distributed could have provoked violence against Jewish students and, therefore, his speech was not protected under the First Amendment. Freedom of Speech, they maintained, was not an absolute right and must be balanced by other equally compelling interests—in this case, the rights of students on campus to be free from intimidation. They also argued that a college community is a voluntary association, and that by agreeing to attend Sunshine State, Martin also agreed to abide by a certain set of rules—in this case, refraining from speech that could provoke violence.

For Discussion

Whose position makes the most sense to you—that of Martin's lawyers or that of the lawyers for the University? Do you think that Martin's lawyers are right in arguing that there are potential dangers to limiting freedom of speech, even if that speech is hurtful or offensive? Why or why not?

What is a Person?

In contemporary moral philosophy a debate has arisen about what exactly a person is. This question gets to the heart of ethics because most moral philosophers argue that we have certain moral obligations towards persons that we don't have towards non-persons. We have seen in our discussion of deontology, for example, that Kant makes a distinction between persons and things, arguing that the former must always be treated as ends in themselves, while the latter can be used merely as means. The question of what exactly a person is, however, is not as obvious as it might seem.

Some moral philosophers have argued that the term "person" should be used synonymously with human being. If this is the case, we still need to ask ourselves what a human being is. Is it simply a matter of appearance? But then what about someone born with numerous physical defects? Are they still human beings even though they may not have all the characteristics we normally associate with human beings? Perhaps a human being is simply a matter of having a certain genetic make-up. The problem here is that creatures such as chimpanzees have a genetic code that is 98 percent identical to human beings, but we would probably not classify them as human.

Other philosophers like John Locke focus on self-consciousness as the essential quality that distinguishes persons from non-persons. Locke defined a person as "a thinking intelligent Being, that has reason and reflection, and can consider itself as itself, the same thinking thing in different places and times, which it does only by that consciousness, which is inseparable from thinking, and as it seems to me essential to it" (*Human Understanding* 2.27.9). Thus a person for Locke is a living being conscious of itself as persisting over time and therefore having preferences about its own future.

The problem with Locke's understanding of personhood, of course, is that, based on his criteria, there may be persons that are not humans and humans that are not persons. For example, some highly evolved animals such as great apes or dolphins would have to be considered persons, while an irreversibly comatose patient or a baby would not be. Similarly, it might be possible in the future to create an artificial life form that is capable of meeting Locke's criteria for personhood. Would such a "being" then be entitled to the same respect and consideration as any other person?

A similar problem arises when we apply this criterion to the status of the fetus, as those in favor of abortion argue that the fetus is not a person, because it is not self-conscious, while those opposed to abortion argue that the *potential* for self-conscious awareness should be enough to convey personhood. There are difficulties, of course, with both positions. Advocates for abortion have to explain why the fetus should not be considered a person, while a newborn baby, which is equally lacking in self-consciousness, should be; on the other hand opponents of abortion have a difficult time explaining how a single-cell organism with no mind to speak of could possibly be considered a person.

Other possible criteria for personhood proposed by moral theorists include the following:

- the ability to engage in rational thought.

- the ability to make free choices.
- the ability to have projects and plans.
- the ability to use language.
- the ability to experience pleasure and pain.
- the presence of a soul created by God.

Unfortunately, each of these criteria presents its own unique set of problems that must be addressed. If we accept the first three of these criteria, then fetuses, babies, and the severely mentally handicapped would not be considered persons. If we use sentience—the ability to experience pleasure and pain—as our criterion, then animals would also be persons. Finally, the equation of personhood with the presence of a soul may appeal to religious believers, but would certainly not satisfy agnostics or atheists.

In the discussion of rights theory, the definition of personhood becomes extremely important. As we shall see, proponents of this theory argue that the basic rights of all persons must be respected. Once we resolve what these basic rights are, however, we still need to return to the even more difficult question of what constitutes personhood.

What Are Rights?

As Americans we are inundated with talk about rights. We hear constantly about the right to life, the right to freedom of speech, about women's rights, gay rights, even about the right to die. Indeed most of our moral dilemmas are shaped and framed by rights talk in one form or another. But what exactly are human rights anyway?

Moral rights are claims or demands that individuals and groups can make upon other members of a society, and which therefore impose a duty or obligation on the actions of others in that society. For example, if one has the right to freedom of speech, this means that other members of the society do not have the right to interfere with this speech; if one has the right to a free public education, this right imposes an obligation on others in the society to pay the costs of that education. Moral rights also entail a certain obligation on the part of the rights holder about how that right is to be exercised. For example, even though one might have a right to freedom of speech, one also has an obligation to exercise that right in a responsible manner. According to rights theory, therefore,

an act is right if, in performing it, one does not violate the basic rights of others.

In the event that two or more rights are in conflict, we are obligated to act in such a way as to ensure that the most important rights will be respected.

Historical Background of Moral Rights Theory

The idea of moral rights became popular in political thought in the 17th and 18th centuries. John Locke, who is considered by many to be the father of moral rights theory, developed a concept of natural rights, which he believed to be derived from God. In his work, *Two Treatises of Government*, Locke identified three fundamental natural rights—life, liberty and property. Locke's position had a great impact on the faculty fathers of the United States. Thomas Jefferson, most notably, took many of the ideas found in the writings of Locke and used them as the basis for his "Declaration of Independence":

> We hold these truths to be self-evident; that all men are created
> equal, that they are endowed by their Creator with certain un-
> alienable rights, that among these are Life, Liberty and the pur-
> suit of Happiness—That to secure these Rights, Governments
> are instituted among Men, deriving their just powers from the
> Consent of the Governed, that whenever any Form of Govern-
> ment becomes destructive of these Ends, it is the Right of the
> People to alter or abolish it, and to institute new Government,
> laying its Foundations on such Principles, and organizing its
> Powers in such Form, as to them shall seem most likely to affect
> their Safety and Happiness.

According to classical rights theory, moral rights are bestowed by virtue of humanity and have nothing to do with who you are, your social status, your citizenship, or the laws of the state. Moral rights according to this tradition are also understood to be "unalienable." They can't, in other words, be given or taken away. A rights holder may at times choose not to exercise the rights he possesses (for example, refraining from speaking when he has the right to) or to allow someone else to exercise a right for him (as a parent would do for his child or a severely mentally handicapped adult relative).

Not long after the Declaration of Independence was written, the newly established United States of America became the first country to enumerate specific rights for all of its citizens. These rights were introduced in a series of amendments to the Constitution proposed by James Madison. In 1791 ten of these amendments were ratified and became the Bill of Rights. Among the rights recognized by the Constitution of the United States are the following:

- the right to freedom of religion, speech, press, and assembly, as well as the right to petition the government (1st amendment).
- the right to keep and bear arms (2nd amendment).
- the right to protection from unreasonable search and seizure (4th amendment).
- the right to due process under the law, protection against self-incrimination, limits placed upon eminent domain (i.e., private property taken for public use) (5th amendment).
- the right to trial by jury and other rights of the accused (e.g., the right to receive information about the nature and cause of the accusation, the right to confront witnesses, the right to have a defense lawyer provided (6th amendment).
- the prohibition of excessive bail, as well as cruel and unusual punishment (8th amendment).

Rights theory advanced considerably when on December 10, 1948 the General Assembly of the United Nations adopted the Universal Declaration of Human Rights, declaring the rights contained therein as "a common standard of achievement for all peoples and all nations." Among the rights recognized by this document that go beyond those enumerated by the U.S. Constitution are:

- the right not to be held in slavery and servitude (Art. 4).
- the right not to be subjected to cruel, inhumane, or degrading treatment or punishment (Art. 5).
- the right to seek and enjoy in other countries asylum from persecution (Art. 14).
- the right to marry and found a family (Art. 16).
- the right to social security (Art. 22).
- the right to work, to choose one's own employment, to be protected against unfavorable work conditions, to be protected against unemployment, the right to equal pay for equal work and the right to join labor unions (Art. 23).

- the right to rest and leisure, including limitations placed upon working hours and periodic holidays with pay (Art. 24).
- the right to a standard of living adequate to support oneself and one's family (Art. 25).
- the right to education, including free primary education, and equal access to higher education (Art. 26).
- the right to freely participate in the cultural life of one's community, to enjoy the arts, and to share in the benefits of scientific achievement (Art. 27).

Moral Decision-Making Using Rights Theory

Preparatory Stage: Determine what specific rights human beings possess (feel free to use the U.S. Constitution and the U.N. Declaration of Rights as guides) and to whom these apply

Step 1: Identify the action being considered.
Step 2: Determine if the action being considered violates anyone's basic rights.
Step 3: If it doesn't, then the act is morally right; if it does, then the act is morally wrong.

Human and Legal Rights

A distinction that should be kept in mind is the difference between human and legal rights. Legal rights refer to those rights found within existing legal codes. Such rights are dependent upon the passing of a law which grants these rights to individuals within a given society and protects them under the laws of that society. For example, the right to receive a high school education is a legal right granted by the laws of the United States, but which would not be recognized in some other societies. Human rights, on the other hand, are rights which transcend the particular laws of a given society. The UN Universal Declaration of Human Rights, for instance, claims that all human beings have the rights to life, liberty and the security of person (Article 3), the right not to be held in slavery or servitude (Article 4) and the right not to be subject to torture, inhumane or degrading treatment or punishment (Article 5). Each of these rights is considered by those who drafted this document to be a human right existing independently of any individual legal code.

It should be noted that there are some political thinkers, such as legal positivists, who believe that the only rights that truly exist are those that originate within a legal system, and that therefore, human rights are fictions. "No laws," they argue, "no rights." The problem with such a limited perspective on rights is that it would seem to prevent any redress to those living in societies with unjust laws. Legal positivists, for example, would have had a difficult time arguing against the existence of apartheid in South Africa, because the laws in that country clearly sanctioned discriminary treatment of black South Africans. In such cases it becomes necessary to appeal to rights which transcend the specific legal codes, in order to protect individuals being treated inhumanely within their own countries.

Negative and Positive Rights

In recent times a somewhat controversial distinction has been made between negative and positive rights. Negative rights are rights not to be interfered with by government or fellow citizens. The rights to freedom of speech, religion, and assembly, which are included in the Bill of Rights of the U.S. Constitution, are negative rights of noninterference because they prevent others from interfering with the actions protected by these rights. Such rights, however, do not obligate others to help us exercise our rights. Positive rights—also known as entitlements or welfare rights—are rights which impose obligations on others to provide goods or services to which the rights holder is entitled. Rights to health care, education or employment are examples of positive rights.

While liberal thinkers tend to support the idea of positive rights, other political thinkers, such as libertarians, argue that there are no such things as positive human rights. Although they are adamant in their defense of negative rights, libertarians believe that so-called positive rights are nothing more than infringements upon the rights of those who are expected to provide entitlements. As Ayn Rand, the philosophical guru of many in the libertarian movement, writes:

> Any alleged "right" of one man, which necessitates the violation of the rights of another, is not and cannot be a right.
>
> No man can have a right to impose an unchosen obligation, an unrewarded duty or an involuntary servitude on another man. There can be no such thing as "the right to enslave."
>
> A right does not include the material implementation of that

right by other men; it includes only the freedom to earn that implementation by one's own effort.

Observe, in this context, the intellectual precision of the Founding Fathers: they spoke of the rights to the pursuit of happiness—not the right to happiness. It means that a man has the right to take the actions he deems necessary to achieve his happiness; it does not mean that others must make him happy....

The right to property means that a man has the right to take the economic actions necessary to earn property, to use it and dispose of it; it does not mean that others must provide him with property.

The right of free speech means that a man has the right to express his ideas without danger of suppression, interference or punitive action by the government. It does not mean that others must provide him with a lecture hall, a radio station or a printing press through which to express his ideas.

Any undertaking that involves more than one man, requires the voluntary consent of every participant. Every one of them has the right to make his own decision, but none has the right to force his decision on the others...(113-114).

As we have seen, libertarians believe that the only obligation that we have to others is that of forbearance or refraining from interfering with their rights. They argue that there are no other obligations that we have towards our fellow citizens.

Liberty and Its Limitations

The First Amendment to the Constitution enumerates certain basic liberties that all human beings possess and which are protected by law. Among these are the right to freedom of religion, speech, press, and assembly. The wording of this amendment might lead one to conclude that these liberties are absolute, but this has never been the case. Since the time that the Constitution was written, there have been numerous questions about the scope of individual liberty and its limitations.

In 1859, the English utilitarian philosopher, John Stuart Mill, attempted to address this question in his work, *On Liberty*, which has come to be viewed by many as the greatest treatise on human liberty ever written. Mill's basic premise in *On Liberty* is that government has the right to limit people's freedoms only when it is necessary to prevent them from causing harm to others. As Mill wrote,

The only purpose for which power can be rightly exercised over any member in a civilized community, against his will, is to prevent harm to others. His own good, either physical or moral, is not sufficient warrant. He cannot rightfully be compelled to do or to forbear because it will make him better to do so, because it will make him happier, because, in the opinion of others, to do so would be wise or even right. There are good reasons for remonstrating with him, or reasoning with him, or persuading him, or entreating him, but not for compelling him or visiting him with any evil in case he do otherwise. To justify that, the conduct from which it is desired to deter him must be calculated to produce evil to someone else. The only part of the conduct of anyone for which he is amenable to society is that which concerns others. In that part which merely concerns himself, his independence is, of right, absolute. Over himself, over his body or mind, the individual is sovereign (9).

Unless they are likely to harm others, Mill believes that people should have an absolute right to do whatever they want. He notes, however, that this principle applies only to competent adults. It does not apply to children or those suffering from serious psychological illnesses.

Mill's "harm principle," on the other hand, would allow for government interference in acts that cause harm to others or which have the potential to cause harm to others—acts such as theft, violence, rape, or drunk driving. Short of that, Mill believes that people have a right to do whatever they want with their lives, even if their actions might cause harm to themselves. Thus, while cigarette smoking, drinking to excess, sky-diving, or eating fatty foods might cause harm to the individual engaged in such behavior, the government does not have a right to interfere, unless it can be demonstrated that other members of the society have been harmed by the behavior. We might forewarn such individuals about the follies of their ways, but we should not interfere with their behavior, no matter how irresponsible it might seem to us.

Mill also believes that individuals need to be protected against, what he refers to as, "the tyranny of the majority." This sort of social tyranny occurs when the majority uses coercive means to compel individuals to conform to its norms of behavior, Mill believes that the majority has even more pernicious ways to control its members:

Society can and does execute its own mandates; and if it issues wrong mandates instead of right, or any mandate at all in things in which it ought not to meddle, it practices a social tyranny more formidable than many kinds of political oppression, since, though not usually upheld by such extreme penalties, it leaves fewer means of escape, penetrating much more deeply into the details of life, and enslaving the soul itself. Protection, therefore, against the tyranny of magistrates is not enough; there needs to be protection against the tyranny of prevailing opinion and feeling, against the tendency of society to impose, by other means than civil penalties, its own ideas and practices as rules of conduct on those who dissent from them; to fetter the development and, if possible, prevent the formation of any individuality not in harmony with its own ways, and compel all characters to fashion themselves upon the model of its own. There is a limit to the legitimate interference of collective opinion with individual independence; and to find that limit and to maintain it against encroachment is as indispensable to a good condition of human affairs as protection against political despotism (7).

In Mill's view the tyranny of the majority is much more dangerous than the tyranny of governments because it is more pervasive and harder to protect oneself against. He believes, therefore, that individuals need as much protection against social tyranny as they do against political tyranny.

Advantages of Rights Theory

Rights theory has a number of distinct advantages that make it one of the most practical and concrete of all the moral theories that we have examined so far. Among these advantages are the following:

Rights theory protects and promotes the value of individuals. Any advocate of rights theory must hold that human persons have intrinsic value and that their interests must be protected from the interference of others. The theory also treats human beings as moral equals, and, therefore, helps prevent discriminatory practices towards members of different races, genders, or sexual orientations. The emphasis on moral equality also makes it an ideal ethical system for democratic societies.

Rights are objective. When rights theory clearly spells out those fundamental rights, such as life, liberty, privacy, and property that must be respected, it provides a clear framework for moral-decision making. Although there may be debate over how to interpret and apply certain rights—for example, whether there should be any limitations placed upon rights such as freedom of speech or religion—at least rights theory gives us a clear starting point for our moral deliberations.

Disadvantages of Rights Theory

As is the case with all of the theories we have examined, there are certain inherent problems with rights theory that have been raised by critics:

There ain't no such thing as rights. Some moral thinkers, such as Jeremy Bentham, have argued that while the idea of moral rights sounds nice, in reality any talk about human rights is nothing more than "non-sense on stilts." Such critics maintain that rights only exist once they have been established by a given society. The idea of natural human rights, therefore, is simply a myth that has no philosophical justification.

Which rights are right? Even if we grant that there are such things as human rights, agreeing on exactly what rights human beings possess is still somewhat difficult. We have seen that many liberals would include the rights to decent housing, employment, and adequate shelter as basic human rights, whereas libertarians would reject these outright. One major problem with rights theory is that its proponents typically do little more than present a list of basic rights without providing an adequate philosophical rationale for why certain rights are fundamental and others are not. Libertarians tend to be better at providing this sort of rationale than liberals, although the number of basic rights they recognized is, not surprisingly, fairly circumscribed.

What are we to do when rights come into conflict? Like duties, rights are prima facie, and therefore may come into conflict with one another. The most famous illustration of this sort of conflict is between the woman's right to privacy and the fetus' right to life. In such cases it is often difficult to determine which right should take priority, and the result has been decades of political battles between abortion rights advocates and their opponents with no real resolution of this question.

For Further Discussion

1. Based on our discussion of moral rights theory in this chapter, answer the following questions concerning the scope of moral rights:

   - Should individuals have a right to health care even if they can't afford to pay for it? If so, who should be forced the bear the large costs necessary for ensuring this right?

- Should people have the right to smoke in enclosed public spaces if they so choose?

- Do only human beings have rights? Or do you think that animals have certain rights as well? If so, what would some of these rights be?

- Should minors have the right to have an abortion without notifying their parents?

- Do future generations have any rights? If so, what are they?

- Should individuals have the right to put whatever information they want on the Internet, even if such information might be a potential threat to public safety?

- During wartime or other times of great emergency, should people be allowed to criticize the actions of the government or, in such specific cases, should limitations be placed upon freedom of speech?

- Is there a right to privacy, and if so, is this right absolute?

- Do indivdiuals of the same sex have the right to get married?

2. The "establishment clause" in the first amendment of the U.S. Constitution specifically states that "Congress shall make no law respecting an establishment of religion or prohibiting the free exercise thereof." Do you think that this clause allows for the following:

    - organized prayer during school hours (those students who feel uncomfortable with this practice are permitted to opt out)?

    - voluntary Bible study and prayer after school on school grounds?

    - the placing of art works or sculptures depicting the Ten Commandments in courthouses?

    - the placing of a nativity scene on town or state property?

    - government funds given to religious organizations to provide services for at-risk populations?

3. The second amendment of the Constitution states the following: "A well-regulated Militia, being necessary to the security of a free State, and the right of the People to keep and bear Arms, shall not

be infringed."

- Do you think that the framers of the Constitution meant this amendment to allow anyone to own weapons?
- Is this right absolute?
- Does this right also allow people to own assault weapons, as the National Rifle Association maintains?

4. The eighth amendment prohibits the use of "cruel and unusual punishment." Does this mean that extreme methods of interrogation (i.e., waterboarding, excessive sleep or food deprivation, etc.) cannot be used against terrorism suspects?

5. Liberty and Its Limitations: According to Mill's "harm principle," which of the following actions would be a legitimate use of government power to regulate the behavior of individuals?

- laws mandating the use of seatbelts in cars.
- laws preventing teens from drinking alcohol.
- laws requiring individuals to drive at certain speed limits.
- laws preventing adults from using drugs such as marijuana or hashish.
- laws preventing adults from using hard drugs such as heroin and cocaine.
- laws preventing access to certain sites on the Internet deemed dangerous

Sources and Further Reading

Donnelly, Jack. *Universal Human Rights in Theory and Practice.* Ithaca, NY: Cornell University Press, 1987.

Feinberg, Joel. *Rights, Justice, and the Bounds of Liberty.* Princteon, NJ: Princeton University Press, 1980.

Harpham, Edward, ed. *John Locke's Two Treatises of Government: New Interpretations.* Lawrence, KS: University Press of Kansas, 1992.

Locke, John. *On Human Understanding.*

—. *Two Treatises of Government.* New York: New American Library, 1965.

Libertarian National Committee. *National Platform of the Libertarian Par-*

ty. Adopted: July 2, 2006.

Luytgaarden, Eric van de. *Introduction to the Theory of Human Rights.* Utrecht: Utrecht University, 1993.

Lyons, David. *Rights.* Belmont, CA: Wadsworth, 1979.

Machan, Tibor. *Individuals and Their Rights.* LaSalle, IL: Open Court, 1989.

Meldon, A.I. *Human Rights.* Belmont, CA: Wadsworth, 1970.

Mill, John Stuart. *On Liberty.* Indianapolis, IN: Hackett, 1978.

Nickel, James. *Making Sense of Human Rights.* Berkeley: University of California Press, 1987.

Rand, Ayn. "Man's Rights." *Capitalism: The Unknown Ideal.* New York: Penguin, 1966.

Shue, Henry. *Basic Rights.* Princeton, NJ. Princeton University Press, 1980.

Simmons, *The Lockean Theory of Rights.* Princeton, NJ: Princeton University Press, 1992.

Waldron, Jeremy. *Theories of Rights.* New York: Oxford University Press, 1984.

10

VIRTUE ETHICS

Case Study: An Attempt at Self Improvement

Valerie Carolan has come to an impasse in her life. She is currently a sophomore at Michigan State University and is enrolled in the university's rigorous pre-law program. One day she wakes up in her dorm room and realizes that her life is a mess: sprawled out in the bed next to her is some guy that she doesn't even know who smells really bad. Her head is pounding like a jackhammer from all the drinking she did the previous night and she realizes that she too must look (and smell) absolutely horrible from her wild night on the town.

As she gets out of her bed, she recalls the events of the previous evening– how she chose to go out partying instead of studying for the philosophy exam that she will have to take in one hour; how she drank to excess, and in a state of intoxication flirted outrageously with a dumb jock she met in a bar; how she fought with her roommates, who objected to her bringing a strange guy into their dorm room. She is pretty sure that she had some kind of physical intimacy with the jock in bed with her, but can't remember if they had sexual intercourse, and, if they had, whether they had used any kind of protection.

Getting out of bed quietly, she quickly puts back on the clothes from the previous evening that are scattered on the floor around her and slips out into the common area of her dorm room. Sitting there in the living room are Valerie's roommates who clearly are enraged with her. Her roommates tell Valerie that they have had it with her. They say that lately she has been ignoring all of her responsibilities and spending most of her time partying and picking up guys. If she continues in this way, they warn her, she will probably fail out of college and ruin her life. They also are tired of her explosive anger, her laziness and her sloppiness around the dorm. They tell her that, unless she makes a conscious effort to work on some of these character defects, they will have no option but to ask for her to be kicked out of the dorm.

Upon hearing this, Valerie explodes in a fit of rage and storms out of the living room. Walking through the campus, her head still pounding severely, Valerie reflects back on her life, acknowledging that for some time now her life has been spinning out of control. Although she is still angry at her roommates for their lack of support, she admits to herself that she needs to radically transform her character if she is going to make it through the next two-and-a-half years of college.

For Discussion

What are some of the qualities of her character that Valerie needs to change if she wants to live a happy and productive life? What kind of program of character transformation would you recommend Valerie undertake in order to turn her life around? Be specific in your recommendations.

Imagine that Valerie has decided not to work on her character flaws, but rather chose to move into a single dorm room so that her behavior would not affect anyone else. Would her behavior in this case still be morally problematic? Why or why not? What would a utilitarian or a deontologist have to say about this?

Doing and Being

Most of the ethical theories that we have examined have focused on the rightness or wrongness of specific actions. The basic moral question for a utilitarian or deontologist would be the same: "What should I do?" In answering this question, the utilitarian or deontologist would point to specific rules or principles that ought to be used to guide moral action.

In opposition to these approaches, virtue ethics focuses on the character of the moral agent, and asks a more difficult—and perhaps more profound—question: "What kind of person should I become?" Instead of providing rules or principles, the virtue ethicist would focus instead on specific qualities of character—or virtues—that a good person ought to possess. "Be truthful, be compassionate, be generous," the virtue ethicist would respond, and you will probably behave the correct way in most circumstances. We do good, in other words, because we are good.

Virtue ethicists, therefore, argue that moral action has nothing to do with the rightness or wrongness of specific acts, but rather with the character of the person who performs the act. Thus the position of virtue ethics maintains that *an act is right if it is performed by a person of virtuous moral character.*

To help illustrate this point, let's imagine that you have a grandfather who is universally acknowledged to be an exemplary human being. In all the years that you have known him, you have never heard him utter an unkind word or perform an unjust action. In fact, he always goes out of his way to treat everyone he meets with charity, benevolence, and sensitivity. He is, in other words, a person of the highest moral caliber.

One day, however, the police come to your door and tell you that your grandfather has been accused of murdering an acquaintance and that the weapon used in the crime was found in your grandfather's possession. What would you think about hearing this from the police? Your natural reaction would be to think that there is some kind of mistake—that your grandfather couldn't have committed the act described or that, if he did, he must have had a very good justification. In the end, your views are proven to be correct. In fact, what actually happened was that your grandfather was helping a friend move his gun collection and, while he was removing a handgun, it accidentally discharged, killing his friend. You knew that your grandfather must have been innocent, because you knew what kind of character he had, and you also knew that a person with that kind of character would never kill anyone intentionally

Thus, rather than spending time trying to figure out what kinds of actions are right or wrong, the virtue ethicist looks to exemplary individuals like grandpa—or perhaps even more saintly individuals, like St. Francis, Mother Teresa, Gandhi, or Martin Luther King—and tells us instead to develop the specific qualities of character that these kinds of people possess.

Aristotle's Virtue Ethics

Like utilitarianism and deontology, virtue ethics has taken on many different forms in recent times. Almost all contemporary virtue ethics approaches, however, owe a considerable debt to the theory of the virtues that was developed by Aristotle over 2,300 years ago. Aristotle was born in Stagira, Macedonia in 384 BC. After studying with Plato at his Academy he returned to Macedonia to act as a tutor for Alexander the Great. In 335 B.C. he went to Athens for a second time to found his own school, the Lyceum, and taught there for the next twelve years. After the death of Alexander, Athens rebelled against Macedonia, and Aristotle was forced to flee Athens to avoid being put to death. He died one year later in 322 B.C.

Aristotle certainly was one of the greatest thinkers in Western Civilization and wrote on almost every topic imaginable: biology, logic, poetics, rhetoric, politics, physics, and metaphysics. We know that he also wrote at least two, and perhaps three, different works on ethics. For our purposes the most relevant of these works is the *Nicomachean Ethics*, which contains his most complete treatment of the virtues. Because the work was written in the form of lecture notes and reflects the Athenian culture in which he was living, Aristotle's *Ethics* seems at first like a rather dubious vehicle for developing a virtue ethics for the 21st century. And yet, if we can get beyond his archaic language, we will find a work that is surprisingly engaging and extremely relevant to our own times.

Human Happiness

Aristotle's approach to ethics has been described as teleological in nature. A teleological approach is one that looks to the end, goal or purpose (*telos*) of human existence in order to determine how we ought to act. For Aristotle, everything in the universe had a purpose, so it is hardly surprising that he would think that human action would have some kind of purpose as well. Because Aristotle, like most of his Greek contemporaries, believed that this purpose was somehow directed towards the attainment of happiness, he begins his investigation of ethics with an examination of the nature of human happiness.

The highest good for human beings, Aristotle believes, is the attainment of happiness (*eudaimonia*) and it is the attainment of happiness that is the goal of everything we do in life. Aristotle goes on to define happiness as "activity of the soul in accordance with virtue (*arête*)." It is the life of virtue, in other words, that leads human beings to the happiness they ultimately seek. Although Aristotle speaks of different types of virtue—physical, intellectual and moral—it seems clear that he believes moral virtue is that human excellence that most directly contributes to happiness.

The Golden Mean

So if happiness is attained through the acquisition of moral virtue, the next logical question becomes: how is this virtue to be attained? Most moral action, Aristotle says, concerns itself in one form or another with the emotions. "By emotions," he specifies, "I mean appetite, anger, fear, confidence, envy, joy, affection, hatred, longing, emulation, [and] pity" (*Ethics* 1105b 20-22). For Aristotle there is nothing either good or bad about the emotions themselves; what is good or bad is how we choose to act upon them in a particular situation. The role of reason, therefore, is not to eliminate the emotions, but rather to regulate them, so that they do not get out of hand or lead us into trouble.

But what exactly is the right way for reason to control the emotions? Aristotle uses the analogy of a good work of art. For a Greek, the perfect work of art is one in which nothing can be added to or taken away from it. Think of a great work of art such as Michelangelo's David or Beethoven's Ninth Symphony, for example: there is a harmony to these kinds of works that makes them seem totally complete in themselves. We wouldn't want the artist to add or take away anything from them for fear of ruining their perfection. This kind of excellence in a work of art, then, would be destroyed through excess or defect. Excess and defect are also possible in the realm of human action: we can get too much or too little food, too much or too little exercise—both of which would prove harmful to a human being. In the realm of human action, then, Aristotle thinks that we ought always to strive for what the Latins called the "golden mean" (*aurea mediocritas*) or, to put it in his own language, a mean state between two extremes, excess and defect, with respect to action and emotion:

> Virtue, then, is a state of character concerned with choice, lying in a mean, i.e , the mean relative to use, this being determined by a rational principle by which the man of practical wisdom would determine it. Now it is a mean between two vices, that which depends on excess and that which depends on defect; and again it is a mean because the vices respectively fall short of or exceed what is right in both passions and actions, while virtue finds and chooses that which is intermediate (*Ethics* 1107a)

To put this in simpler terms, virtue for Aristotle is nothing more than a means between two extremes (an excess and a defect) with respect to a particular action or emotion.

Illustrating the Virtues

A few examples will help to illustrate Aristotle's theory of the virtues. Let's take the virtue of courage as our first example. Aristotle defines courage as a mean state between the two extremes of cowardice and recklessness with respect to the emotion of fear. A courageous person in this view feels just the right amount of fear when confronted by a dangerous situation; the cowardly person feels much more fear than he should; the reckless feels much less. Aristotle's treatment of courage might strike some as a bit dubious since many of us have been led to believe that a courageous person is someone who actually feels no fear at all. But if we take time to analyze the nature of courage we shall see that Aristotle's view actually makes much more sense than our popular notion of courage.

Imagine for instance that you and a friend are passing a building that is on fire. The building is being rapidly consumed by flames, but the local fire department is not yet on the scene. On the second floor of the building a child is crying out for help from an open window. How would a courageous person respond in such a situation? We know that a cowardly person would probably avoid getting involved for fear of being burnt alive. If you were a coward, you would probably argue that it is best to wait for the fire department to arrive, since they are trained to handle this kind of emergency. In the meanwhile, however, the trapped child will have been burnt alive. Another option is for you to rush into the burning building without a moment's hesitation or forethought, battle the smoke and flames, and try to climb up to the second floor to rescue the trapped child. Even if you managed to reach the child under these conditions, it is not certain that you would be able to carry him out of the house before the roof or stairway collapsed. Both you and the child would end up dead, and all of your heroic efforts would have been in vain. While some might describe your actions as courageous, Aristotle would correctly observe that you were in fact foolhardy rather than courageous—that is, that you didn't have the right amount of fear that you should have had in such a life-threatening situation.

So if you were a truly courageous person what would you do in this kind of situation? First, you would quickly size up the extent to which the house is being burned, the location of the child, and the resources that are available. If the child could in fact be saved by rushing into the house, you might risk it even though there was a chance that you yourself might be trapped; if there is no chance of saving the child that way, you would look for another option. If the child was small enough, for example, you might have him jump out the window into your arms, or if a neighbor was at hand (and there was enough time) you might have the neighbor get a sheet to use as a safety net. Whatever option you chose, it is certain that you would still feel some degree of fear—at the very least for the child whose life is in danger. Aristotle is certainly correct then, when he maintains that a courageous person, unlike a foolhardy one, feels fear. He just isn't crippled by it the way a coward would be.

Another important virtue for Aristotle is that of generosity, which he describes as a mean between the extremes of extravagance and stinginess with respect to the giving and taking of money. A stingy person is someone who exceeds in taking but is defective in giving. We can think of a miserly old person—Dickens' Scrooge, for example—who is excellent at making money from his dealings with other people, but who is horrible at giving it away, even for a good cause.   Once again, we might be tempted to think of a generous person as one who gives without thought to anyone in need, but for Aristotle this would be an extravagant person, not a generous one. This kind of person, he says, exceeds in giving but is defective in taking. I have known people, for example, who, filled with the spirit of Christian charity, have given away much of their money to worthy causes or individuals in need. Unfortunately, many end up not having enough left to pay their monthly bills, and are forced to borrow money from friends or family to survive. This kind of person, while appearing to practice the virtue of generosity is actually not virtuous at all, since he gives from other people's pockets rather than his own.

Finally, for Aristotle, even-temperedness is a means between the extremes of short-temperedness and apathy with respect to the emotion of anger. The even-tempered person is not that individual who never gets angry under any circumstance. There are certainly occasions when even the most mild-mannered person would demonstrate extreme anger—when a great injustice has been committed, for example. If he was protecting the life of someone he loved his anger might even compel him to lash out with great violence. At all times, however, he directs the correct amount of anger towards precisely the right object in order to accomplish his goals. The short-tempered person on the other hand responds to many of life's adversities with an excessive degree of anger and often directs it at the wrong object. He might, for example, be humiliated at work by his boss. Instead of directing his anger at the appropriate source (his boss), in the right way (preferably in private) and to the right degree (firmly but not in a shrill or volatile manner), he takes his hostility out on his wife and children, towards whom his anger should not be directed at all.

In the *Nicomachean Ethics*, Aristotle provides an extensive list of virtues that he believes are essential for morally good persons to possess. Each of these virtues basically follows the same format described above. They are understood to be means between two extremes, an excess and a defect with respect to a particular emotion.

Acquiring Virtue

We have seen that for Aristotle all human action aims at happiness and that happiness is connected to a life of virtue. If we accept this starting point of Aristotelian ethics, the next question that should automatically be asked is: how do we learn to become virtuous men and women?

In answering this question Aristotle begins by making the distinction between intellectual virtues, such as practical wisdom, and moral virtues, such as courage, generosity, and the like. Intellectual virtues, he believes, are acquired by education; moral virtues by habit. In other words, Aristotle rejects the notion that a child—or even an adult for that matter—can be taught to be good:

> Argument and teaching, I am afraid, are not effective in all cases: the soul of the listener must first have been conditioned by habits to the right kind of likes and dislikes, just as land must be cultivated before it is able to foster the seed. For a man whose life is guided by emotion will not listen to an argument that dissuades him, nor will he understand it. How can we possibly persuade a man like that to change his ways? And in general it seems that emotion does not yield to argument but only to force. Therefore, there must first be a character that somehow has an affinity for excellence or virtue, a character that loves what is noble and feels disgust at what is base (*Ethics* 1179b 23-31).

The problem as Aristotle sees it is that if a person does not already have a virtuous disposition, then he will not be open to moral education, and if he already has a virtuous disposition then he really doesn't need it.

All human beings, Aristotle believes, are born as blank slates, without either good or bad characters. The character that we ultimately develop is a result of upbringing, and this character can get better or worse depending on the specific kind of training that we receive growing up. Parents, therefore, need to mold the characters of young people in the right way to help them become virtuous adults. Aristotle uses the example of learning to play a musical instrument to demonstrate the right way to go about training young people to be moral. Certainly no one believes that he can simply teach a child to become the next George Gershwin. To learn to play the piano well, a child must constantly practice, starting with the most basic notes and working his way to the most complex scales. At first the child will inevitably stumble over the notes he is learning to play, but eventually, if he is diligent enough and practices every day, he will be able to play the piano as though it was second nature to him. According to Aristotle, a similar process is involved in training a child to behave virtuously. When a child is first being trained, he finds it difficult and often has trouble doing what his parents expect of him. As he constantly practices specific virtues, such as honesty and generosity, he will eventually find it easier and easier to behave virtuously, until it becomes extremely difficult for him to even conceive of engaging in any kind of vicious behavior.

ARISTOTLE'S VIRTUES

Virtue	Excess	Defect	Emotion
Courage	Cowardice	Foolhardiness	Fear
Temperance	Self-Indulgence	Insensibility	Desire for pleasure of the body (eating, drinking, sex)
Generosity	Extravagance	Stinginess	Desire to give money to those who need it
Proper Pride	Vanity	Humility	Desire to receive great honors
Good Temper	Irascibility	Apathy	Proneness to anger
Wittiness	Buffoonery	Boorishness	Desire to amuse others
Modesty	Bashfulness	Shamelessness	Susceptibility to shame

A Program of Moral Perfection: Benjamin Franklin

In his *Autobiography*, American writer, inventor, and diplomat, Benjamin Franklin offers a description of his rise from a poor tradesman to a giant in the pantheon of American history. Franklin was encouraged to write his autobiography in order to inspire young men to strive to rise above the limitations of their social condition and achieve the kind of success that he had in his own life. The work itself became so famous that it has served as a kind of bible of self-improvement for generations of Americans.

An important part of Franklin's program of self-improvement was an attempt he made at a fairly early age to become morally perfect. Describing his motivations for this project, Franklin writes:

> ...I conceived the bold and arduous project of arriving at moral perfection. I wished to live without committing any fault at any time; I would conquer all that either natural inclination, custom, or company might lead me into. As I knew, or thought I knew, what was right and wrong, I did not see why I might not always do the one and avoid the other (120).

Franklin soon discovered that it was easier to desire to live a moral life than it was to live one. Like all individuals who make resolutions to improve their lives, Franklin realized that the habits of a lifetime were not soon broken, and that the vices that he had cultivated often proved too strong to overcome. He concluded that "the mere speculative conviction that it was in our interest to be completely virtuous was not sufficient to prevent our slipping; and that the contrary habits must be broken, and the good ones acquired and established, before we can have any dependence on a steady, uniform rectitude of conduct" (121).

The way he set about to achieve moral perfection was to examine the ideas of the great moral theorists throughout the ages to see what specific virtues they advocated practicing. Putting his own distinctly American spin on the project, Franklin soon devised a list of 13 virtues that he deemed most applicable to his project of moral self-improvement: temperence, silence, order, resolution, frugality, industry, sincerity, justice, moderation, cleanliness, tranquillity, chastity, and humility.

Because Franklin believes that it would be too arduous an undertaking to attempt to master all these virtues at once, he resolved to fix upon one of them at a time. Once he mastered one of the virtues, he would then move on to the next, until he acquired all 13.

But Franklin also determined that he needed a method for determining that he was progressing in mastering each virtue. And so he created what might be called a virtue log:

> I made a little book to which I allotted a page for each of the virtues. I rul'd each page with red ink, so as to have seven columns, one for each day of the week, marking each column with a letter for the day. I cross'd these columns with thirteen red lines, marking the beginning of each line with the first letter of one of the virtues, on which line, and in its proper column, I might mark, by a little black spot, every fault I had found upon examination to have been committed respecting the virtue upon that day.
>
> I determined to give a week's strict attention to each of the virtues successively. Thus in my first week, my great guard was to avoid even the least offense against Temperance, leaving the other virtues to their ordinary chance, only marking every evening the faults of the day (124-125).

Thus Franklin turned his attention week by week to each of his thirteen virtues, determined to have no black marks in the column devoted to that week's specific virtue. If he could succeed in this endeavor, he thought, he would have strengthened that virtue and weakened its opposing vice.

Benjamin Franklin doesn't usually get recognized as a great moral theorist, and this is perhaps justified given that his account of his own program of moral improvement only takes up about seven pages of an autobiography otherwise devoted to his business practices. And yet Franklin offers us a unique step-by-step method for moral improvement that is unique in Western thought. His method, in fact, is perfectly applicable to anyone seeking to improve his or her moral character.

Developing Your Own Core Virtues

All virtues can be divided into two different kinds: those that pertain to other people (other-regarding virtues) and those that pertain to oneself (self-regarding virtues). The former help to make social life possible; the latter enable us to develop character traits that lead to personal integrity and moral wholeness.

The following is a typical list of both kinds of virtues:

Other-Regarding Virtues	Self-Regarding Virtues
Benevolence	Courage

Civility	Industriousness
Compassion	Moderation
Kindness	Self-Control
Dependability	Self-Discipline
Justice	Self-Reliance
Generosity	Cleanliness
Honesty	Pride
Loyalty	Self-Respect
Tolerance	Humility
Sensitivity	Dignity/Honor
Friendliness	Prudence
Discretion	Modesty
Reliability	

According to virtue ethics, part of the moral maturation process that human beings go through involves identifying—as both Aristotle and Franklin did—core virtues that one voluntarily chooses to practice. Some of these virtues may have been imposed upon us as children or by the particular cultures in which we live, but most virtue ethicists believe we have some control over whether or not we choose to continue to embrace these virtues as we mature.

One way of identifying those virtues that are important to you is to ask the following question: If you were a parent, which of the above virtues would you want your children to possess? Focusing on your actual or future children is a good way to develop a list of virtues that is personally significant, because it offers the opportunity for you to step back and think about this question in a slightly more objective way than if you focused on your own character.

Once you've approached the issue in this way, you can then put the spotlight more directly upon yourself. You've come up with five or ten virtues that you'd want your children to possess. Are these the same set of virtues that you would have selected if asked to choose for yourself? Not surprisingly, most people normally tend to answer this question in the affirmative. If that's also the case for you, then the next obvious question would be: what are you doing to strengthen these virtues in your own life?

As we saw from our discussion of Aristotle, moral virtue is all about practice, practice, practice. Once your core virtues have become habitual and no longer represent a struggle for you, morality in this system basically takes care of itself. The person of good moral character doesn't have to agonize over specific moral decisions, because he or she is now flying on a kind of ethical auto-pilot. It's not a matter of knowing what the right thing to do is in a specific situation, but rather allowing your character to guide you into being the kind of person—kind, compassionate, discreet, loyal, just, etc—that you've always wanted to be.

Moral Decision-Making Using Virtue Ethics

Preparatory Stage: Make a list of those virtues which you believe contribute to human excellence. You may want to make use of the lists on the previous page to assist you in this effort.

Step 1: Practice each of these virtues regularly until they become habitual (i.e., second nature).
Step 2: Add more virtues as needed until you develop the kind of optimal moral character to which you aspire.
Step 3: There's no need to worry about specific moral actions, since a person with good moral character will automatically act in the right way without great effort.

Contemporary Virtue Ethics Theory

One of the most interesting attempts in recent times to revive a theory of the virtues has been carried out by Alasdair MacIntyre in his provocative work, *After Virtue*. In this work, MacIntyre offers an extremely persuasive critique of the state of contemporary moral philosophy and an impassioned argument in favor of the return to a more classical approach to ethics with an emphasis on the virtues.

MacIntyre begins his account by describing human life as a "narrative quest." This quest, he maintains, represents a search for self-fulfillment—that is, for our own good as human beings—and it is the virtues that support us in this quest. Our understanding of the virtues, however, is not shaped by ourselves but by the particular tradition to which we belong. Thus MacIntyre points out that in Homeric culture, in which the paradigm of excellence was the warrior, the virtue of courage would be paramount, while in Aristotle's own time the paradigm was the Athenian gentleman, and, therefore, the virtue prudence would take priority. He goes on to demonstrate that the specific virtues that were considered important in first century Christian circles, in Jane Austen's England, and in Benjamin Franklin's America likewise prove to be fairly distinct from one another. Each tradition, according to MacIntyre, will have its own catalogue of the virtues and these catalogues will often be in conflict with one another:

> Homer, Sophocles, Aristotle, the New Testament and medieval
> thinkers differ from each other in too many ways. They offer us
> different and incompatible lists of the virtues; they give a differ-
> ent rank order of importance to different virtues; and they have
> different and incompatible theories of the virtues. If we were
> to consider later Western writers on the virtues, the list of diver-
> gences and incompatibilities would be enlarged still further; and
> if we extended our inquiry to Japanese, say, or American Indian
> cultures, the difference would become greater still. It would be
> all too easy to conclude that there were a number of rival and
> alternative conceptions of the virtues, but, even within the tradi-
> tions which I have been delineating, no single core conception
> (181).

MacIntyre's conclusion is that there are no universal set of virtues
that can be applied to all people at all times. Each culture or tradition's
set of virtues will be unique to that tradition, and fully understandable
only from within that particular tradition.

The analysis of the virtues developed by MacIntyre points to a significant problem that must be addressed before we can continue any further. MacIntyre suggests that any attempt to develop an ethics of virtue
would necessitate an acceptance of cultural relativism, and that the terms
"virtue" and "universal" must be understood to be mutually incompatible. This sort of tradition- or context-bound account of the virtues has
consequently been criticized by those who are looking for a more universal ethic that can transcend cultural boundaries. Martha Nussbaum,
summing up these objections, writes,

> For this reason it is easy for those who are interested in support-
> ing the rational criticisms of local traditions and in articulating
> an idea of ethical progress to feel that the ethics of virtue can
> give them little help. If the position of women, as established by
> local traditions in many parts of the world, is to be improved, if
> the traditions of slave holding and racial inequality, if religious
> intolerance, if aggressive and warlike conceptions of manliness,
> if unequal norms of material distribution are to be criticized
> in the name of practice reason, this criticizing (one might eas-
> ily suppose) will have to be done from a Kantian or Utilitarian
> viewpoint, not through an Aristotelian approach (33).

James Gustafson goes even further when he accuses thinkers like MacIntyre of adopting an anti-rational and sectarian approach to ethics that ultimately forfeits any relevance beyond the particular tradition of the moral theorist (92).

In an effort to respond to some of these objections, attempts have been made in recent times to demonstrate the universality of certain virtues. Jean Porter, for example, argues that there are certain virtues, such as practical wisdom, courage, and temperance, that are "perennial" and which would be recognized as virtues in every culture. "They are perennials," she writes, "because they are integrally related to the human capacity to sustain a course of action, based on overarching principles, ideas, plans or goals" (61).

Similarly, Martha Nussbaum attempts to refute the claim that Aristotelian virtues are essentially relativistic. She argues rather that Aristotle presents a single objective account of the human good, which is derived, not from a local tradition, but from something shared in common by all human beings. That which we all share in common are "spheres of experience" that are perfected by virtue. She selects eleven spheres from Aristotle and says that each of these spheres is essential for human living. Nussbuam thus argues that Aristotle's account of the virtues actually transcends cultural boundaries (36).

Advantages of Virtue Ethics

Among the strengths of virtue ethics as a moral theory are the following:

Virtue Ethics places an emphasis on creating good human beings. People typically do not behave morally simply because they have accepted certain rules or principles of moral behavior, but rather because they are good human beings. The basic premise of virtue ethics is that if we can work to transform our characters—to become, in other words, virtuous individuals—then we will consistently act in a morally good manner. On the other hand, all the rules and principles in the world will not help us if we have morally defective characters.

Virtue Ethics places an emphasis on human motivation. In recent years many moral philosophers have begun to reexamine virtue ethics as a preferable alternative to modern moral theories. One of the greatest strengths of virtue ethics is that, unlike some of the other moral theories that we have examined, it focuses not just on actions, but on motivation as well, and therefore, provides a richer account of moral action.

Consider the following example used by James Rachels:

> You are in a hospital recovering from a long illness. You are bored and restless, and so you are delighted when Smith arrives to visit. You have a good time chatting with him; his visit is just the tonic you needed. After a while you tell Smith how much you appreciate his coming—he really is a fine fellow and a good friend to take the trouble to come all the way across town to see you. But Smith demurs; he protests that he is merely doing his duty. At first you think that he is only being modest, but the more you talk, the clearer it becomes that he is speaking the literal truth. He is not visiting you because he wants to, or because he likes you, but only because he thinks that it is his duty to "do the right thing," and on this occasion he has decided it is his duty to visit you—perhaps because he knows of no one else who is more in need of cheering up or no one easier to get to (Rachels, 187; adapted from Stoker).

The point of this example is that, while there is nothing wrong with Smith's actions, we would rightly be disappointed with his motives. We would much rather have a friend act out of loyalty or devotion—out of virtue, in other words—than simply out of a cold, calculating, rational sense of duty.

Disadvantages of Virtue Ethics

Although a character-based approach to ethics has some distinct advantages over the rule-based approaches that we have examined in this text, it also has some distinct disadvantages as well. Among the most notable weaknesses of virtue ethics are the following:

Virtue Ethics fails to provide adequate moral guidance. Let's imagine that you are faced with a moral dilemma about whether or not to end life support for your ailing parent. The best advice that virtue ethics could offer you would be to do what a person of good moral character would do in this situation, which doesn't provide much concrete guidance in these kinds of crisis situations. It doesn't tell us which acts are virtuous and therefore ought to be performed in this specific circumstance.

What virtues should we adopt? In his work, After Virtue, Alasdair MacIntyre argues that all virtues are relative to the specific cultures in which they exist. Aristotle's list of virtues, Macintyre maintains, would look very different from that of Thomas Aquinas, Benjamin Franklin or Jane Austin. It would appear then that there is no universal set of virtues that would apply to all individuals. We are left to wonder which virtues we ought to adopt when deciding on how best to improve our moral characters. In the end, there could be as many different sets of possible virtues as there are different cultures—or even individuals—in the world.

For Further Discussion

1. Case Studies in Virtue Ethics

    a. Cheating in Chemistry

    Nakeem and Alex are two college students who are also star players on their college basketball team. Because they are teammates they have spent a great deal of time together at practice and at games. Occasionally they socialize together, though usually as part of a larger group of friends.

    The two also happen to be taking advanced chemistry together, because they are both Pre-Med majors. Doing well in the course is considered essential for admission into a decent Medical School—a goal to which both Nakeem and Alex aspire. During their final exam for the class Nakeem spots Alex cheating. He wonders whether he should report Alex to the professor.

    What virtues or vices would be manifested if Nakeem reports Alex for cheating? What do you think Nakeem should do?

    b. Paying for an Abortion

    Park City, Utah. 1957. Midge and Sara are high school juniors who have been best friends since the second grade. Last year Sara became involved in a sexual relationship with Lou, a senior. Midge has never fully approved of the relationship, because she finds Lou untrustworthy. Being a supportive friend, however, she has kept her criticisms of the relationship to herself.

    One day Sara comes to Midge in tears, telling her that she is pregnant and that her boyfriend will leave her if she doesn't have an abortion. Because abortion is illegal, Sara has to go to a "special" doctor, who, she has been told, will perform the procedure in secret for $200. Neither Sara nor Lou have that kind of money themselves, but Sara knows that Midge can get the money from her father if she lies to him about what it will be used for. She implores Midge to help her. If she doesn't have the abortion, Sara tells Midge, her reputation will be ruined, her parents will disown her, and she will be abandoned by her boyfriend.

What virtues or vices would be manifested by Midge getting the money for Sara? What do you think Midge should do?

   c. Squealing on Your Brother

For some time now, Kurt Zimmer has been aware that his brother, Gunther, has been hanging out with a crowd of friends who may be involved in illegal activities. Recently, there has been a rash of break-ins in the neighborhood, and thousands of dollars worth of personal property has been stolen. Police suspect that the culprits may be a gang of local youths.

One day, while Kurt is looking in his brother's dresser for an item of clothing that he lent him, he opens the bottom drawer and discovers several items of expensive jewelry that he knows Gunther could never afford. Kurt quickly closes the drawer and leaves the room, extremely disturbed by what he has seen.

Not knowing what to do, Kurt confides in the most virtuous person he knows, his good friend, Norbert Dressner. Norbert tells Kurt that he has a duty to report his brother and his friends to the police to prevent any more households from being robbed. The situation comes to a climax, when police come to the house and directly ask Kurt if he knows anything that could help them solve the case of the break-ins.

What virtues or vices would be manifested if Kurt decides squeal on his brother to the police? What do you think Kurt should do?

2. Dilemmas in Virtue

   a. In the Gospels, Jesus espouses a radical ethic of selfless love (*agape*) that involves sacrificing your own well-being at times to care for those in need. This ethic is reflected quite clearly in the Sermon on the Mount and the parable of "The Good Samaritan." Do you think it makes sense to practice the virtue of selfless love, particularly if it leads to sacrifice and suffering for yourself? Since this virtue is so central to the teachings of Jesus, does a rejection of the importance of selfless love also imply a rejection of Jesus' teachings?

   b. In liberal societies, tolerance is a fairly important virtue, since it allows individuals to pursue their own good without interference from others. Do you think tolerance is a virtue worth practicing? If so, does this mean you shouldn't criticize or interfere with behavior you find morally repulsive?

c. Aristotle argues that true happiness comes from a life of virtue. And yet some of the most virtuous people in history have met fairly tragic ends—e.g., Socrates, Thomas More, Gandhi, Martin Luther King...The list goes on and on—while many extremely vicious people seem to lead perfectly delightful lives. Do you think there is a valid connection between happiness and virtue?

d. Many commentators have in recent years been bemoaning the death of civility among younger generations. Using expressions like "please" and "thank you," holding the door open for people behind you, and saying excuse me when you burp at the table may seem unimportant, they argue, but, in fact, the loss of such common courtesies is symptomatic of a basic lack of repect and concern for other human beings, and, therefore, is an important moral issue. Do you think a lack of basic courtesy and civility is simply a sign of changing cultural norms or do you agree that it represents a serious character defect?

e. To gossip is to say something negative about someone else behind their back. Gossiping is also something that just about everyone does to make social interaction much more pleasant. And yet, the fact that most people would never want the content of their gossiping to get back to the object of their gossip suggts that most people intuitively recognize that there is something at least morally problematic about gossiping. Do you think gossiping is simply a neutral cultural practice or do you think it's a vice? If a vice, do you think that you could ever completely stop gossiping?

3. On the Virtue's Committee. This exercise is best done in a group. The aim is to see whether you and your fellow "committee members" can arrive at a consensus on a set of universal virtues:

You are the parent of a seven-year-old child, who has been selected to enter a new experimental school that is opening in your community. The three hundred children that will be enrolled in this school come from a wide variety of cultural backgrounds and reflect a rich diversity of race, ethnicity, and religious practices. The school will also have at least forty students enrolled whose families have recently immigrated from other countries from around the world.

The school was founded because parents in the community wanted an educational environment that would train their children in important virtues. The only problem is that, because the children come from such a wide variety of backgrounds, it has been difficult to reach a consensus on what these virtues should be.

To solve this problem a committee made up of parents, administrators, teachers, and community and religious leaders has been formed to devise a list of twenty virtues that everyone agrees are essential for all the children in this school to practice on a consistent basis.

You have agreed to serve on this committee. List at least five virtues that you believe are essential to include on this list. Be sure to give an explanation as to why you think each virtue deserves to be included on the master list.

Sources and Further Reading

Adams, Robert Merrihew. *A Theory of Virtue*. New York: Oxford University Press, 2006.

Aristotle. *Nicomachean Ethics*. Trans. Martin Ostwald. Englewood Cliffs, NJ: Prentice Hall, 1962.

Baron, Marcia. "Varities of Ethics of Virtue." *American Philosophical Quarterly* 22 (1985): 47-53.

Crisp, Roger and Slote, Michael, eds. *Virtue Ethics*. New York: Oxford University Press, 1997.

Darwell, Stephen, ed. *Virtue Ethics*. Malden, MA: Blackwell, 2003.

Foot, Phillipa. *Natural Goodness*. Oxford: Oxford University Press, 2001.

Franklin, Benjamin. *Autobiography*. New York: Houghton Mifflin, 1923.

Hardie, W.F.R. *Aristotle's Ethical Theory*. Oxford: Clarendon, 1968.

Hunt, Lester H. *Character and Culture*. Lanham, MD: Rowman and Littlefield, 1997.

Hursthouse, Rosalind. *On Virtue Ethics*. Oxford: Oxford University Press, 1999.

—. *Virtues and Vices*. Berkeley, CA: University of California, 1978.

Keenan, James F. "Proposing Cardinal Virtues." *Theological Studies* 56 (1995).

MacIntyre, Alasdair. *After Virtue*. Notre Dame, IN: University of Notre Dame Press, 1984.

Nussbaum, Martha. "Non-Relative Virtues: An Aristotelian Approach." *Midwest Studies in Philosophy* 13 (1988).

Porter, Jean. "Perennial and Timely Virtues: Practical Wisdom, Courage and Temperance." *Changing Values and Virtues*. Ed. Dietmar Mieth and Jacques Pohier. Edinburgh: T. and T. Clark, 1987.

Sherman, Nancy. *Aristotle's Ethics: Critical Essays*. New York: Rowman and Littlefield, 1999.

Slote, Michael. *From Morality to Virtue*. New York: Oxford University Press, 1992.

Taylor, Richard. *Pride: The Lost Virtue of Our Age*. Amherst, NY: Prometheus, 1995.

——. *Virtue Ethics: An Introduction*. Amherst, NY: Prometheus Books, 2001.

Wallace, James. *Virtue and Vice*. Ithaca, NY: Cornell University Press, 1978.

THE GREAT THEORIES: PUTTING IT ALL TOGETHER

Case Study: The Family Home

Mrs. Grace Hightower has inherited a house on a piece of waterfront property in the town of Crystal Cove, Florida, which has been in her family for several generations. She has lived in the house for over thirty years, has raised three children in it, and has had many wonderful memories associated with the house and property. A widow for over ten years with a very limited income, Mrs Hightower was planning to spend her remaining years living in the house and eventually, after she died, pass the property on to her children.

In recent years the town of Crystal Cove has grown significantly and has witnessed an influx of extremely wealthy retirees, seeking to live by the seashore. Unfortunately, there is a limit to the amount of seafront property available in the town because most of it is either owned already by people like Mrs. Hightower or is sensitive wetlands that the town has been trying to preserve. A local developer has convinced the mayor of the town, Bill Shuntell, that if he was allowed to build high rise condominiums along the coast, the taxes generated from these properties could help lift the town out of its fiscal difficulties and pay for projects, like school construction, that would benefit all the citizens of the town. In addition, the presence of so many wealthy retirees living in the town would be a boon to local restaurants and businesses that have not been doing so well in recent years.

Convinced of the importance of the project to the town, Mayor Shuntell immediately went before the town board and got them to agree to use a legal proceeding known as eminent domain to condemn and take over about fifty acres of waterfront property with about forty houses on them. Eminent domain has been used for some time by towns around the country to take over private property that is considered blighted in order to allow for public projects that would benefit all citizens (e.g., the creation of roads, hospitals, schools); in more recent years the Supreme Court has ruled that eminent domain could be used to allow towns to take over property for commercial development like the project being considered by the town of Crystal Cove.

On July 14, 2006, Mrs. Hightower was informed by the sheriff of Crystal Cove that her property would be taken over by the town at the end of the year and her house demolished to make room for the new condominiums. She would be compensated for her loss in the amount of $240,000, which is what the town determined that her house and property were worth. Upon hearing this news, Mrs. Hightower immediately went on the offensive, speaking out publicly against the mayor and the town board members and beginning legal proceedings against the town.

Although Mayor Shuntell knew that the law was on his side, he also knew that Mrs. Hightower was becoming a lightening rod for opposition to his plan and that her court case could potentially hold up his building project for several years. He decided that the smartest thing to do would be to neutralize Mrs. Hightower's opposition to the plan as quickly as possible.

One day in September, Mayor Shuntell goes to Mrs. Hightower's house to make her an offer she can't refuse. Mayor Shuntell says that he has a plan to spare Mrs. Hightower's house and those of some of her immediate neighbors. His plan is to move the development project further south along the coast. This would mean that other people's property would be taken by the town, but, because of their limited incomes, the people in this area have less political clout than Mrs. Hightower and her neighbors, and, therefore, would be less successful in raising opposition to the project. Moving the project south also means that the town's beautiful wetlands, which house numerous species of wildlife, would have to be destroyed to allow for building. Mayor Shuntell goes on to say that, if Mrs. Hightower promises to publicly support the new development plans, she can keep her home; if not he would keep the project location as is and her home would be condemned by the town.

Mrs. Hightower is torn by this proposition. On the one hand, she loves her home and wants to be able to spend the rest of her life living in it. On the other hand, she is philosophically opposed to the way that the Mayor is using eminent domain and has a great deal of pity for the new families that would now be affected by the move of the project location, many of whom she knows personally. She is also horrified that the town's wetlands would now have to be sacrificed so that she could remain in her home.

For Discussion

What would an ethical egoist, utilitarian, deontologist, rights

theorist, and virtue ethicist say is the right thing for Mrs. Hightower to do in this situation? Be sure to explain why each moral theorist would argue the way they do using the specifics of the case.

Although there are many more moral theories than those presented in this text, we have focused on five of most significant theories in the field of ethics. Let's sum these five up one last time for comparison sake:

Ethical Egoism: "An act is morally right if, more than any other alternative available at the time, it brings about the greatest amount of good, or happiness, for oneself."

Utilitarianism: "An act is morally right if, more than any other alternative available at the time, it brings about the greatest amount of good, or happiness, for all those who are affected by the act."

Deontology: "An act is morally right if, and only if, it accords with a universal rule that all can follow."

Rights Ethics: "An act is morally right if, and only if, in performing it, one does not violate the basic rights of others."

Virtue Ethics: "An act is morally right if, and only if, it is performed by a person of virtuous moral character."

After examining these theories in some detail, and going through case studies and exercises to illuminate them further, you should have formed some intelligent opinions about these theories. One or two of these theories in particular may have struck you more forcefully than the others. It's now time for you to take a stand and specify which of these theories you think has the greatest degree of validity and would provide the best possible guidance for your own moral decision making.

Of course, it may be the case that none of the theories presented in this book resonates very much with you. As I have already mentioned, however, there are many more moral theories in the field of ethics than the few that we have focused upon in this text. If you haven't been able to commit yourself to any moral theory by this point, you will have to keep exploring the field of ethics in order to find a more satisfactory theory.

It might also be the case that you feel it necessary to combine different theories—for example, virtue ethics and deontology or utilitarianism and rights theory—in order to create an ethical system that makes the most sense to you. Or you may want to pick and choose different aspects of the theories that we have examined in an attempt to hobble together a more satisfactory theory. Feel free to try this as well.

The point is that ethics is a creative science, one that demands both critical reflection as well as imaginative insight. If you keep thinking about moral issues in a creative way, you may even come up with your own original moral theory, one that is as innovative and original as anything the great moral theorists profiled in this text were able to devise. If nothing else, your reflections on moral theory will probably serve to make you just a bit more ethical in your daily life…and that can't be such a bad thing now, can it?